Victory Or Death

Victory Or Death

Blockchain, Cryptocurrency & the FinTech World

PATRICK L YOUNG

DV BOOKS

VALLETTA

To:

Beata for being Brilliant,

Lucy for being Lovable

& Toby for being Terrific.

"Those things which I am saying

now may be obscure,

yet they will be made clearer

in their proper place."

Nicolaus Copernicus

Contents

By The Same Author

Capital Market Revolution!
The New Capital Market Revolution!
The Promiscuous Investor
Single Stock Futures A Traders Guide
The Exchange Manifesto
The Exchange Invest 1000

As Editor:

An Intangible Commodity
The Gathering Storm
DLT Malta – Thoughts from the Blockchain Island

"It was the best of times, it was the worst of times, it was the age of wisdom, it was the age of foolishness, it was the epoch of belief, it was the epoch of incredulity, it was the season of Light, it was the season of Darkness, it was the spring of hope, it was the winter of despair, we had everything before us, we had nothing before us."

Charles Dickens "A Tale of Two Cities"

Acknowledgements

Given it was only a decade ago that the currently somewhat omnipresent phrase "fintech" was coined, it is perhaps ironic that this tome marks 20 years since the first bestselling book on the topic of er, fintech.

Having written "Capital Market Revolution!" during late 1998 through the first two months 1999... it is a measure of the extent to which the world has changed in the past decade that when the original Capital Market Revolution! hit the book stores on July 1st 1999, it was at once derided by many established market participants. Yet the book sold out wherever it was stocked. That data dichotomy led to a clear conclusion: this was a tome whose time had come!

In the old world of supply chain management, the publishers manifestly failed to keep up with demand for more than 6 months as the news of the revolution swept across the globe. Frustrating doesn't even start to surmise the mood of being in the digital world but with information flow ruled by old analogue publishing processes!

At the same time, criticisms of the tome gradually fell away. The predictive record of CMR! frankly astonished me... having written every last word of it! Within a short time the best of the then nascent digital marketplaces grew to dominance and while the legacy exchanges looked powerless to survive the digital onslaught. At the time, my life could not have been busier, touring the globe expounding the messages of the revolution and endeavouring to assure legacy markets that they could survive but they needed to change – and quickly.

We witnessed a remarkable process across the years, and it is perhaps intriguing that I can frame both the title of this tome and the development of the revolution by looking at a microcosm of the conference world.

With the dawning of the 20th anniversary of the original "Capital Market Revolution!" it was clear to me how much was apparently understood and yet, at once, how widely misunderstanding surround a great deal of the componentry which makes up our fintech future. Thus I was inspired to break down some key issues and show – in what I hope may interest some more lay readers as well as pure play financial folk – how best to understand key developments in fintech and its close cousins the Blockchain and cryptocurrency.

Meanwhile, it is amusing to look at the way the world of fintech has changed since I originally began writing "Capital Market Revolution!" in 1998!

On the cusp of the millennium, those thinking coherently about the future of markets, were, frankly a relatively modest parish of people scattered across the globe. As you may recall optimistic voices were being drowned out by the millennium bug mafia whose scaremongering proved wildly exaggerated. Meanwhile, the phrase 'fintech' itself was not even introduced until 2009, a full ten years after my original tome "Capital Market Revolution!" had become a bestseller in its niche.

Nowadays fintech has become more mainstream and there is a great deal more written about the subject. That said, my major inspirations on the topic tend to remain those who were in the modest cadre of folks who could see the revolution at a time when dial up modems were gradually giving way to a first wave of permanent connections (this was a solid generation before wifi) and none of us interacted via WhatsApp or Facebook as both were some way in the future – I salute those who were active on the web whether it was circa 1994 like myself or soon thereafter...

To that end, Professor Richard "Doc" Sandor deserves a first mention as he was the man who mapped out the electronic futures exchange in a magnificent 1970 paper which was discussed in

"Capital Market Revolution!" to which he generously contributed the excellent Foreword.

Without a doubt the man who has achieved the most in market structure during the time since "Capital Market Revolution!" was published is Jeffrey Sprecher, a man who is not merely a brilliant entrepreneur but somebody who has proven himself a magnificently adept hand at scaling up his business and running a Fortune 500 company with many entirely justified plaudits for his great achievements. I am totally honoured that Jeff agreed to give of his time to contribute the foreword to "Victory or Death?" Thank you, Jeff. Your contribution means an enormous amount to me and I know I am just one of many who salute the incredible achievements you have made along with your brilliant team at ICE.

Sadly some of those who featured in the original "Capital Market Revolution!" 20 years ago are no longer with us. I miss the utterly unique Rory Collins who took the ASX electronic but rarely a day goes by without remembering one of his many magnificent one liners…. Indeed in Rory's own words I believe we are in 'heated agreement' about his many great qualities.

Sadly Paul-Andre Jacot is just one of many characters from the SFOA and Burgenstock no longer with us, he too was a larger than life presence in the world of exchanges and derivatives.

Leonard Bonello will I am sure be pleasantly surprised to find himself mentioned here but beneath that unassuming manner is a brilliant legal mind and a wise counsellor – thank you Leonard for making the transition to Malta such a success for myself and Beata and thank you for helping inspire me during the writing of this book. Likewise, I appreciate your input to the board of Blockchain Malta along with the wonderful Max Ganado and our association's lead globetrotter, Ian Gauci. Thank you all.

Joseph Antony Debono and Tyron Baron have been hugely helpful and provided welcome input to this process, thank you!

In the gestation of this book, many have assisted, mostly unwittingly! To that end nobody can be held responsible for this tome apart from me but in some way all of the following have been a source of inspiration, thank you

Mike Aikins, Ulf Axman, Simon Barberi, Robert Barnes, Tyron Baron, Mark Beddis, Ann Berg, Paul Bowes, Jeremy & Julie Braithwaite, Dimitri Burshtein, Mike Charlton, Joe Christinat, Theresa DeLuca, Theo Dix, Dusan Dobromirov, Joshua Ellul, Kenneth Farrugia, David Feltes, Stuart & Maggie Gill, David Hardy, Alasdair Haynes, Lee Hodgkinson, Colin Howard, Peter Jessup, Huw Jones, Josh King, Tom Krantz, Peter Lenardos, Kelly Loeffler, Michael Mainelli, Claire Miller, Rebecca Mitchell, Otto Naegeli, Ken O'Brien, Jim Oliff, Bob Paul, Michal Polasik, Jake Pugh, Peter Randall, Andy Ross, John Serocold, Jonathan Seymour, Steve Smith and Martin Watkins, Ryan Wells are just a selection of those who have particularly helped with this tome.

I hugely appreciate the assistance of the staff at DV Advisors, Project Vistula and Revolution Market Capital particularly my ace sidekick Aleksandra Kaluzna.

Likewise I owe a debt of gratitude to all the subscribers of Exchange Invest, thank you for supporting the bourse business daily newsletter (ExchangeInvest.com).

A special word to the members of the Casino Maltese and the staff who have always taken an interest – particularly Marguerite, Pauline, Selina and Nico.

Finally this tome wouldn't happen without two very special women I am blessed to have in my life. Thanks Lucy for being my Mum and thank you Beata for being brilliant. (Go WonIT!).

It seems nobody can escape CSR at any time these days so as a disclosure, I have played CSR2 during the production of this tome (go Scorpions Elite... NatMo, please improve reliability) and indeed it must be recorded for the business form of "CSR," some Pokemon are likely to have been harmed in the production of this book.

Preface

Victory or Death?

Preface by Jeffrey Sprecher

I have a view that most people are resistant to change. Few of us like change, no matter how adventurous we think ourselves. It is hard and it is uncomfortable, but also inevitable.

During the formative years of my career, I was an avid reader of Forbes magazine, back in the era when the magazine's founder, Malcolm Forbes, was its editor and publisher. A larger than life character, Forbes crisscrossed the world aboard his "Capitalist Tool," a Boeing 727 that allowed him to mix with tycoons and royalty in their salons or at his homes, which included a villa in Marrakech and the Château de Balleroy in Normandy.

A Forbes feature from that period has stuck with me. I think about it often because it fundamentally altered the way I deal with the inevitable change that comes in business, or in life. The article told the story of people who seemingly died on the operating table but were miraculously revived after their EKG flatlined. When these patients were interviewed about their ordeal, most of them, amazingly, described a common experience.

They painted a picture of a warm white light drawing them in. As the light pulled on them, they spoke of flashbacks to the happiest, most important moments in their lives: a first kiss, their wedding day, the birth of a child. At the same time, this cohort of unexpected survivors also hearkened back to moments of profound sadness: the loss of a family member, getting fired from a job, or hurting someone they loved.

At the end of their lives on earth, these people were recalling their most important moments, the best of times and the worst. It's a humbling thing to think about, made more so by the fact that the common list of memories were also ones of profound change. Malcolm Forbes passed away in 1990, but the lesson in that article lives on: the most important moments of your life, for good or ill, are the moments of change that often will define your life.

At about the same time I was getting involved in the exchange industry, in the late 1990's, Patrick L Young saw enormous change ahead for our industry. Capital Market Revolution!, his first book, earned popularity throughout the world of exchanges, and beyond, as one of the first tracts to foretell much of the transformation ahead for the world's market structure.

The changes that Patrick predicted were indeed a revolution. The situation we face today is a lot different but still encapsulates a fascinating period of change for us all. Change is all around us, and the pace remains considerable., but it's easy to become complacent.

Today, an upstart competitor, or a player from outside of the industry, can readily step into a market where things are relatively organized. The number of participants remains relatively low, so you needn't knock on many doors to draw attention to your disrupting new innovation. It's a lot easier to start something credible today than it was at the turn of the century, when everything was disorganized, before the Capital Market Revolution really got underway.

The ongoing fintech revolution is real, which is why our company, and others, are always analyzing, building, or buying new technologies and new systems. There's an urgency to remain on top, on being at the cutting edge, or a risk of being displaced.

When I peel back the layers of what makes Intercontinental Exchange tick we are, at our core, a database operator. While that doesn't sound as sexy as saying you're a derivatives exchange, it accurately describes funneling data into a database and, organizing it, and distributing it out, the process repeating itself on billions of data points every day.

Even while we invest in new distributed ledger technology through Bakkt, we also constantly improve a legacy technology that is also a distributed database: You can trade on any of our markets and you will see on your iPhone that you did a trade. Your broker knows it, you know it, and we know it. What just happened? We have distributed this database, and done it transparently, in real time.

While the process of change is proving relentless, whether revolutionary or evolutionary, we also have an acute need for more financial education, including better understanding both about the markets themselves and also the technology driving the databases powering our investment processes. As professional risk managers, we need the best possible information for all of our customers who are using data to manage risk twenty four hours a day, every day of the year.

In this, his newest book, Patrick looks more broadly across the realm of technologies applicable to financial markets as well as organizational forms that are shaping the industry of the future. He brings a unique viewpoint to help understanding of how banks and exchanges are positioned for the coming decades, as well as offering an expert take on the impacts of much-discussed — and little understood — technologies such as Bitcoin, cryptocurrency and blockchain.

As with everything Patrick writes, this book is a thought provoking read about the present, with a healthy side order of history. From Cotrugli to Copernicus, we venture on a journey through the ages and across the globe, not only from east to west but, indeed, out of this world into the orbiting planets. One notable aspect to all the challenges of change: in each age, change helped us progress through an arc of increasing prosperity for all, expanding in tandem with dramatic innovations and investment in financial infrastructure.

As I ponder Patrick's perspectives, among the fascinating issues is how many people are more comfortable with technology than they are with the institutions of government. Millennials seem to put more faith in the mysterious personage of Satoshi Nakamoto than they do in the U.S. Federal Reserve. That's a change we can't afford to ignore. Commuters avoid boarding a taxi that has been inspected and certified with a medallion, but will gladly take a ride from an unknown driver because a range of peers assigned him an average of 4.79 stars. There is this comfort and trust with technology which, in many ways, redefines many aspects of business.

If my firm doesn't fulfill the needs of our customers, somebody else will, with a database that may be centralized or decentralized. We wake up every day appreciating the simple maxim that Patrick has adopted as the title of this book, just as much today, from our position on the list of the Fortune 500, as we did when we were a startup. At the same time, we look forward to reading and digesting Patrick's considered thinking at the apex of markets and technology.

Welcome to a world where, amid the complexity of modern organizations and technology, one simple maxim remains valid when it comes to servicing clients or facing the consequences. How my company, and yours, approaches change will be pivotal to our fortunes. As Patrick refers in the title, typical of his "PLY" pith, the binary challenge can be simply termed "Victory or Death!"

Jeffrey Sprecher
Founder, Chairman and CEO, Intercontinental Exchange
Chairman, New York Stock Exchange

Preamble

"The new always happens against the overwhelming odds of statistical laws and their probability, which for all practical, everyday purposes amounts to certainty; the new therefore always appears in the guise of a miracle."

Hannah Arendt

They say don't change a winning formula…but you have to keep ahead of the game.

Building on the legacy of "Capital Market Revolution!" and its slightly later edition "The New Capital Market Revolution!" was always going to be a challenge. In time other books have emerged …indeed this is my tenth tome (between those fully written or 'merely' edited). However people still get in touch by various means including email and approach me at conferences around the world to say how much they enjoyed, or were at once terrified or thrilled by, the pulsating tone which – often with angry denouements – discussed the future of markets in an online world.

To give an idea of how the tome was ahead of the curve, the actual term "fintech" only emerged a decade after the "Capital Market Revolution!" the first bestselling book of the topic, was published!

It all began with a rather blunt statement:

"There is nowhere to hide from capital markets. Nobody is safe from the "Capital Market Revolution!" The Capital Market Revolution presents the greatest upheaval ever seen in the fabric of financial markets, and is born of, and driven by, new technology which will ultimately change the lives of every individual on the globe."

…And accelerated from there.

"Reads like a Tom Clancey novel" one early reader remarked and it was not the last such statement. At the same time, back in 1999

"Capital Market Revolution!" was in the vanguard of explaining what technology was doing – and would do – to finance.

Indeed "Capital Market Revolution!" was viewed as so seismic that there are legacy institutions which still struggle to talk to me 2 decades later...

Their loss.

After all since the mid-1990's I was extolling the wonders of the internet and how this would revolutionize currency, finance markets and investment. Highly prescient advice? Quite the contrary, it was just far too ahead of its time for the legacy financial business. Take cryptocurrency for instance: CMR! discussed digital cash yet the cryptocurrency movement has only come anywhere close to approaching a relatively mass adoption for electronic money in recent years.

Indeed as the 20th anniversary of the original best-selling book of fintech approached, it struck me a lot of people are lost trying to slot together various parts of the jigsaw. That inspired "Victory or Death?" I realised there is a need for this volume precisely because a lot of people are still struggling in whole or part with the jigsaw of the fintech revolution. In a busy world we often don't have time to break down major changes and put in perspective what is incremental and what is a more profound movement. This is not what the clearly Paris 1789 inspired rallying cry of CMR! "Liquidity! Accessibility! Transparency!" was all about. Thus it struck me that a little perspective and consideration mixed with foresight might help many citizens and corporations (whether legacy or 'new new thing') to appreciate the big picture moves as well as some incremental factors shaping our world.

Right now a lot of fintech is incremental improvement and a triumph of youthful hubris over real new world advancement – a sound dose of VC investment has propelled many a rather vapid unicorn to date but just as most of the first wave of revolutionaries foundered on the barricades of CMR! Version 1.0, so too the really long-lived truly inspirational fintech players are probably far from fully fledged in most contemporary cases.

Therefore this book is a follow up but not a direct sequel to the original "Capital Market Revolution!" It weaves together a narrative of progress and opportunity through a miscellany of broadly separate standalone chapters. It also attempts to place some key issues in perspective as well as trying to add colour to items which are often overlooked as the carpetbagging end of the consultant classes seek to insert buzzwords into their Powerpoint displays with a view to looking cool. I don't care about looking cool, I have no qualms about upsetting other parties (although I don't seek to rob anyone of their dignity) but I do feel we need to think a bit more coherently about what has been happening, how things are currently and indeed how that affects where the Capital Market Revolution is going...

I will make no apologies where there may be some vestige of lucid brutality in my criticism of incumbents (why not? After 20 years if they haven't got the plot, why waste time on a soft soap response?). However, holistically I retain a huge optimism going forward. Truly transformational technologies surround us and have modified life immeasurably during my lifetime. At the headline, extreme poverty has collapsed from 44% as recently as 1980 to single digit percentages in a world which has grown from 4.4 billion to 7.7 billion people. Famine has become a relative unknown compared to the 1960s and 70s. Similarly the financial world has made great strides. Nonetheless the revolution is in its infancy. Already, behemoths such as Intercontinental Exchange have been built on this revolutionary framework over the past 20 years. Moreover there are many fabulous new financial players emerging. However, elsewhere, we have a lot of technology which is more lipstick on pigs than proven new age digital management thinking and strategy. As for customer service... Right now that looks a touch more neanderthal amongst many achingly trendy fintech entities. A lot of them deploy fledgling Artificial Intelligence solutions to provide customer service. Being charitable, it is successfully artificial...

Capital Market Revolution! hit a specific zeitgeist in the cusp of the 20th century turning towards a new millennium with the dotcom bubble shaking its booty to render the analogue world a historical anachronism that the youth of today finds distinctly impossible to relate to.

This book is, as you would expect, a synergy of considerable thought and analysis. Even more travel went into this tome than its predecessor too. However, as I enjoyed/endured/survived a red eye flight from Amman Jordan to Frankfurt a while back it was clear how much people could do with a spot of clarification that helps paint the macro canvas of fintech. Alternatively, you may consider this book as a form of last call to modernity. Even 20 years into the revolution it is not too late to repent your analogue omissions and get coherently on the digital bandwagon, even as an adopted digital native.

Back in 1999 nobody considered financial technology in huge swathes of the media. One particular London broadsheet city editor at the time relayed a message that he "simply cannot see the point" of the technological future of markets. Such gracious foresight was replicated in many locations which ought to hang their heads in shame now. (Instead they publish what are often gushingly unquestioning profiles of curious 'new age' millennial para-banking operations – essentially exercises in VC balance sheet building in the hope a willing buyer will acquire distribution without worrying too much about prevailing profit). However many others saw the point and I remain grateful to them for their comments to this day: BBC, CNBC in Europe and Asia, PBS (US) and Sky were amongst the tv stations while news media included feature coverage in the Financial Times, The Independent, Time Magazine and the Wall Street Journal to name but a few!

One thing in common between "Capital Market Revolution!" and "Victory or Death?" was an overarching desire to make the book readable and accessible. To that end, I have once again endeavoured to encapsulate a great deal of thinking which can be included within a Transatlantic flight.

Overall the chapters do progress through a narrative, although they are also standalone items to be read in any order which appeals. The book is intended for those with some degree of financial knowledge. I imagine it will appeal predominantly to my fellow professionals in finance and technology – that is both finance and technology as well as those who work in 'fintech.' I won't delve into the endless 'blah-tech' schisms of regtech or insuretech or other somewhat hairsplitting fetishes. This book concerns itself much more about a holistic vision with understanding of separate segments and silos, as opposed to seeking to merely add more buzzwords for the sake of bullshit bingo card ubiquity.

Twenty years on I continue to enjoy the dialogue with the great many people who interacted after reading "Capital Market Revolution!" 20 years ago. Many of you became friends and colleagues – and in some ways your comments may be reflected in this tome. Thank you for your feedback good and bad. As always, I look forward to interacting with you concerning "Victory or Death?" specifically and indeed the holistic progress of the "Capital Market Revolution!" All feedback will be welcome.

From the tiny but gorgeous hill village of Perinaldo, Italy whence "Capital Market Revolution!" was completed, "Victory or Death?" has been creatively inspired by the delightful surroundings of Valletta, in the small but perfectly formed Republic of Malta and many other locales along a fascinating journey.

Patrick L Young
Valletta
Malta
September 2019
Patrick@DerivativesVision.com

"The one thing that's missing, but that will soon be developed, is a reliable e-cash. A method where buying on the Internet you can transfer funds from A to B, without A knowing B or B knowing A."

Milton Friedman, 1999

Background: An Analogue Tale of Nixonian Genius

> *"The circulation of confidence is better*
> *than the circulation of money."*
>
> James Madison

Political observers are quick to deride the 37th president of the United States of America as a result of his intrigues, and extensively documented extracurricular/extra-legal activities which led to his political downfall. However, it is only fair to note that from a pure financial markets perspective, the Nixon Presidency deserves to be seen in perspective as a genuine 'great leap forward' for free markets. Given he was President during the lunar landings, perhaps "one small step for finance, a giant step for markets" is not an unreasonable paraphrase. Indeed he managed two Apollo-sized quantum leaps for markets.

Before you descend into those 'Buzzfeed blues' of feeling suckered at being sidetracked by what may at first glance resemble a vaguely satirical clickbait sentence, or two, I exhort you to read on:

It seems somewhat absurd now to reflect that such was the protectionism of the immediate postwar era, even stockbrokers retained fixed commissions at what are, with the benefit of 20:20 digital markets hindsight, eye wateringly expensive levels. Nixon played a key role in making markets what they are today – cheap efficient and increasingly ubiquitous, with broadly open access. Thanks to the Nixon reforms, the 37th President of the USA powered a remarkable process that has led to capital being allocated more efficiently and swiftly than ever before.

It is a popular, if entirely asinine, remark to assert the evils of derivatives. This omits to see the world much beyond the binary of the analogue and ignores the vast benefits of risk transfer brought by the derivatives revolution. Thanks to Nixon's deregulation of commissions, he drove stockbrokers and investment bankers to find new ways to make money. This involved a paradigm shift away from the cash market equity binary into new and exciting products where greater profit margins could be enjoyed. The iterative process of derivatives evolution would continue apace. In due course, the 'exotic' first tier derivatives became plain vanilla. This propelled further growth in new products. Meanwhile there was a volume surge in the simpler commoditized products as they reached mass market commoditization via being listed on exchanges. True, there have been some dead ends. Banker greed allied with government ignorance produced a near calamitous recession after 2008 for instance. However, the latter could not have been achieved by derivatives alone: It took a good old fashioned government inspired bubble to really fuel the chaos. Cheap money multiplied by leverage and property greed would have inevitably created an ugly bubble without a single CDS or other sophisticated derivative.

However, the key point is the Nixon Presidency drove the world's finances forward thanks to dropping off the gold standard (a more calculated and arguably pork barrel propelled manoeuvre given government addiction to debt in recent decades). Then more specifically Nixon introduced genuine competition for commissions into the rather stuffy world of the broker-exchange 'club' nexus. The reforms themselves took place some months after Nixon's resignation...

Perhaps appropriately, while the already decaying Soviet Bloc was organising militaristic marches in honour of the socialist "Pan European Day of Indolence," May 1st 1975 marked the liberation of American capital markets – and ultimately a rebirth of financial markets – across the world. Amusingly with hindsight, the brokers regarded the great deregulation of commissions as a genuine catastrophe. The financial markets community, privileged with a rather cosseted fixed tariff existence (an irony surely for people of allegedly free market disposition?) also demonstrated a fabulous lack of foresight, firmly believing their post deregulation future would be dismal. This of course leads us to a key conclusion which is, as I have long argued – and the Economist pithily noted more than two decades ago: "Financial services firms are not good at dealing with rapid change."

Thanks to Nixon's foresight, stockbrokers needed to find new sources of revenue. Following Nixon's earlier move to abandon the gold standard, there was a vast opportunity to create new financial instruments. These products have, as noted above, served countless millions of clients throughout the world to benefit from more risk transfer. This has driven a growth in availability of tools which help manage risk and create opportunity throughout financial markets.

In essence therefore the entire process of Capital Market Revolution! finds itself, somewhat perversely, saluting President Nixon. In contrast, Nixon's Presidential legacy is not so richly applauded in the mainstream of political history where it is significantly more contentious, to put it mildly, for reasons which are both well documented and stretch beyond this book's scope.

Perhaps more perversely, there are good grounds for modern financial market practitioners to salute President Kennedy whose term was cut short by his premature demise. Albeit Kennedy is to be applauded for his folly, as opposed to Nixon's whose reforms have delivered a long lasting prosperous upswing. In July 1963 JFK proposed the Interest Equalisation Tax, a temporary balance of payments measure (it actually lasted until 1974). The tax was intended to make it less profitable for US investors to buy overseas assets through a tax on the purchase of foreign securities. However the rather narrow focus of such a de facto withholding duty pushed business overseas. Even in the 1960s when transAtlantic telephony cost around 12 dollars for three minutes (International Direct Dialing – IDD – first connected London and New York in 1970), the process of restricting investors actually drove business away from the US and fuelled trading in US dollars outside North America. The so called "Eurodollar" market for US currency outside America began in 1963 with a bond issue for the Italian motorway network operator Autostrade. However it was not Milan which dominated the European financial marketplace. Rather, the sleeping postcolonial London financial market was awoken from a post imperial torpor to begin a new growth cycle as the global giant of international financial centres it has become today.

Thus in the prehistory of digital markets, at the birth of IDD telephony, lies this analogue preface to our fintech future. Ask anybody today and few would believe we owe a debt of gratitude to Richard Milhous Nixon. In a world of fixed commissions or indeed fixed exchange rates, the opportunity for digital markets would have been significantly less. Through his actions Nixon essentially carved out the opportunity for the new markets which have become the centrepieces of the digital age.

Prelude - The Bürgenstock Lament

> "To know that we know what we know,
> and to know that we do not know
> what we do not know,
> that is true knowledge."
>
> Nicolaus Copernicus

Across the eponymous lake from the city of Lucerne, the 1115 metre Bürgenstock dominates the horizon. At 874 metres sits the Bürgenstock resort, founded in 1873. During Hollywood's Golden Age the resort was on the jetset 'bucket list.' In 1954 Audrey Hepburn married Mel Ferrer in the elegant chapel. Sofia Loren and her husband Carlo Ponti lived in the Villa Daniel for 7 years during the 1960's. The Hammetschwand elevator to the peak viewing area on the mountain was featured in the James Bond film Goldfinger while the Pilatus aircraft factory nearby doubled as a location for Mr Goldfinger's Swiss factory.

In the decades after Sean Connery stayed there, the resort become inadvertently pivotal in the development of financial markets. For over 25 years, in early September, the leading figures in the world of derivatives exchanges would arrive by a cornucopia of transportation. A taxi from Zurich airport takes barely an hour but many preferred the delights of efficient Swiss public transport. First a train to downtown Lucerne, then a walk through the elegant streets to the lakeside. At this point a delightful paddle steamer can transport you across the lake to the small pier and the tour de force: the delightful funicular railway (built in 1888) slices its way almost vertically up the side of the mountain depositing visitors in the resort itself. Once upon a time the great and the good of the exchange industry assembled in the resort for the Bürgenstock Meeting across the early September period when the Labor Day weekend enabled many American executives to spend a few days in Europe and enjoy the mountain airs.

The moods at Bürgenstock meetings were almost invariably optimistic, perhaps aided by the delightfully crisp fresh mountain air and the all round beauty of the local area. Hotels encompassed a panorama from the majestic lake to rolling verdant pasture with sturdy well fed cattle providing a symphony of cow bells as they chewed the cud. However by 1998/99, the exchange delegates at Bürgenstock had an overwhelmingly funereal air. The team from LIFFE – the London International Financial Futures Exchange – were fighting for their survival as a business, having been broadsided by the onslaught of the digital DTB/EUREX marketplace. (See "Capital Market Revolution!" for the story of the "Battle of the Bund"). A few sunny optimists such as Luc Bertrand of the Montreal Exchange (going digital) and Patrick Birley at SAFEX (effectively born electronic) were working on plans to move their markets forward unencumbered by a fear of short-term decimation. Overall, however, the mood was unremittingly gloomy – as befitted an industry where in general digital technology had traditionally been, at best, a peripheral afterthought. Many delegates awoke to that symphony of cowbells in the nearby pastures and pondered when "Big Brother" was going to administer that final shot in the back which would put them and their bourses out of their misery. Thus the years 1998 and 1999 had a spot of Orwellian 1984 fatalism about them. After years of complacency, digital technology threatened the whole world of exchanges and their 'cosy corner' conference circuit across the globe.[1]

1. In the early days of the futures industry during the 1980s one industry wag had termed the Chicago Board of Trade's approach to intercontinental

Somewhat surprisingly to anybody who had witnessed the scenes of relative torpor during the 1999 meeting, twelve months later there was a curious sense of relief on the Bürgenstock…

By 2000, the Bürgenstock meeting convened with the legacy exchange players emerging blinking on top of the mountain in a barely disguised sense of wonder that they had somehow survived the tempest…thus far at least. There was a sense of relief but equally concerns of impending danger on the horizon bubbled just beneath the surface too. It added an almost surreal layer of uncertainty amidst the lush pasture, cowbells and heady mountain air.

The legacy of the 2001 meeting would end up overshadowed by the horrific events of 9/11 which took place just after the event. However on the days leading up to September 9th, overall the mood was upbeat. Exchanges were finding their stride again, the 'for profit' model was winning through as digital technology and new process was rapidly infusing across markets.

It was towards the end of the 2002 meeting that the title for this book emerged from a moment of inspired third party observation on the way to a panel discussion. Back then, when Bürgenstock was a 'must attend' event I had become chairman of the blue riband "Crossfire" panel with industry leaders and assorted experts discussing matters of moment at the climax of the Bürgenstock meeting.

The opening remarks were a flavour of millennial zeitgeist to come. Sweetness and light, cooperation tinged with friendly rivalry were the order of the discussion. That consensus was elegantly obliterated when the Austrian Chief Executive of the German-Swiss EUREX exchange Rudolf Ferscha surmised the challenges facing every vestige of the industry. Addressing the issue of exchange competition, Ferscha looked to the audience and noted the

travel as "Europe on 5000 dollars a day" back when the backpackers' bible was benchmarking the same travels on a paltry five bucks inscription on an historic artwork adorning the walls of the conference hall. It carried a somewhat chilling motto:

"For the sake of the Fatherland, Victory or Death."

As I noted at the time in my online magazine Applied Derivatives: "In many ways, that is the maxim which is most apt not merely for exchanges, now they have abandoned clubbiness for capitalism but indeed for all traders throughout the world. The world of exchange competition is heating up and that is good for traders, as we can increasingly choose which platforms to trade and indeed where to provide and indeed where to find the greatest liquidity."

Or as I put it in "Capital Market Revolution!" ("CMR!"), quoting Hamel & Sampler:

"Somewhere out there is a bullet with your company's name on it. Somewhere out there is a competitor, unborn and unknown, that will render your strategy obsolete. You can't dodge the bullet – you're going to have to shoot first. You're going to have to out-innovate the innovators."

Twenty years on, plus ca change... That statement has been indelibly burned into my memory bank. The realpolitik of a pure "Victory or Death?" showdown is as true at the time of publication in September 2019 as it was in September 2001.

If the "Victory or Death?" observation triggers your inner snowflake, perhaps you are in the wrong industry. The simple truth is that underneath a lot of touchy-feely poppycock and hype in the new millennium, nothing has changed. The world of technologically driven finance is precisely the same cornucopia of human emotion, brutal economic reality and complex politics that has ever been thus. Analogue or digital, competition exists for resources, for talent and above all, for customer business.

When it came to the blunt message of "Victory or Death?" some folks didn't listen. Or, they hubristically inhaled the heady mountain airs and believed it could never happen to them. Perhaps most ironically of all, one victim through pure-play management ineptitude was the Bürgenstock conference itself. The meeting gradually slipped off the agenda of exchange leaders after a period bereft of foresight where some of the board was unable to listen, and the executive proved incapable of coping with change. They simply could not accept a new digital reality: their meal ticket as a leading conference just wasn't guaranteed. In this period of tumult, the whole market structure changed from clubs which were somewhat generous to other clubs and industry associations, towards for profit hard headed capitalist regimes. Think of the irony of that for a moment: Finally the free markets actually arrived in the, er, free markets! As these markets moved away to pastures new, digital redefined the business. In derivatives the fusion of OTC into CCP and on to electronic platforms galvanised a new way of looking at markets. (There will be a myriad of acronyms in this book I will define as elegantly as possible as the story progresses!) Within a few years of Rudi Ferscha's chilling forewarning, Bürgenstock had turned into something more akin to a retirement meeting looking back to the analogue 'good old days' as opposed to the tantalising glimpse of our investment future it had represented for 25 years. Thus the meeting atrophied until a near death experience. Warnings had fallen on deaf ears for several years and the technology changing markets was ignored. When the world moved on, the Bürgenstock meeting was left behind with its parent association the Swiss Futures & Options Association remaining, sadly a shadow of its former self.[2]

Thus one might recall the words of French revolutionary Georges Danton: "La révolution dévore ses enfants" ("The Revolution devours its own children."). He knew that only too well, meeting a sticky end

---

2. Alas as an SFOA board member endeavouring to embrace the digital age, I can recall only too well observing warnings falling on deaf ears. The office holders seemed more concerned with adding oompah bands and Raclette evenings when they needed to renew their content and indeed upgrade their Rollodex for the digital age.

on April 6th 1794, himself a victim of new technology popularised by a revolution: the guillotine...a clear victim of the "Victory or Death?" binary option.

Despite remarkable change in many respects, the process of "Capital Market Revolution!" seen to date has been one where indeed the world has remained remarkably consistent. Those, like myself, noting the time of mass bank upheaval was nigh in 1999, have had to wait 20 years to find a baying mob joining the frey propagating a huge upheaval in the banking system. Banking has remained rather consistently dominant in financial services around the world. However we finally seem to have passed a turning point as "The Peak of Banker Power" chapter discusses. As always, a financial disclaimer: naturally things won't work out quite how the crowd anticipates but in the big picture, banking looks to be in clear difficulty, even before we allow for its own semi-suicidal death wish through scams and schemes which do not enamour the public at large. Nor indeed are many of the millennial 'improvements' on banking likely to demonstrate much greater longevity than the current economic cycle. Then again were many really built to last? Again, they look more like cynical VC backed plays to garner vast market share and then be sold while still broadly profit challenged to the legacy banks they seek to disintermediate.

Nevertheless, the impact of the radical upheaval inspired by the digital network technology on the medieval world of markets is now poised to eat some of its oldest participants – the very banks themselves which have been at the epicentre of finance since the time of the Medicis.

The future of markets will provide rich pickings for some remaining bankers but the core banking model as we know it is now firmly in the sights of the revolution itself. This is hardly surprising. Banking is horribly expensive, frequently profoundly inefficient and banks themselves have comprehensively failed to understand the challenges surrounding them. That's before we factor in often shoddy and sometimes downright corrupt, management. It can be argued, many banks have sought more to cocoon themselves within the protection of a certain regulatory monopoly. Thus they have deployed their lobbying nous and political influence to maintain the status quo at all costs. Whereas exchanges have flourished as they got to grips with the revolution, the eye of the storm is only now positioning itself above the citadels of finance which have become the standard unit of monetary interaction for most of the world. Nowadays exchanges are missing more opportunities than they are capitalising on. Banks, on the other hand, are sailing arrogantly and insouciantly into a gale which makes their ongoing unpopularity in western markets (following their ludicrous bailouts after 2007), look truly like a storm in a teacup.

Ironically, bankers have, as change threatens to overwhelm them, spent a great deal of time taking aim at the more efficient models that surround them. Exchanges and CCP clearing houses have been under fire for their 'excessive' profit. On one metric, the net profit margins achieved by exchanges and clearing houses have indeed proven stupendous in recent years (35-40-% is typical in the major derivatives markets for instance). 'True' capitalism has finally engendered more innovative – and efficient – bourses. Nevertheless, the gaping hypocrisy of the bankers' argument rather beggars belief. Give a banker your money on deposit one day then borrow against it the next and you can easily pay as much as 10 percent (1000 basis points) for the pleasure. When "Capital Market Revolution!" was first launched, various mutual fund managers laughed at my assertion that their 500 basis point ("bps") bid/offer spreads would soon be history. Before the publisher FT Prentice Hall could even satisfy demand for the original CMR!, mutual fund spreads had already dropped precipitously. Early in this century they were already somewhere in the region of 30 bps.

Meanwhile, in later chapters we shall see a pattern that is in some ways unique in terms of scale yet would be unsurprising to a merchant used to the agora in ancient time. , this is the "Age of the Exchange" as much as it is "a bankers' lament."

Meanwhile, those exchanges which banks are keen to revile for their excessive profits will transact a million dollar futures contract for nickels and dimes if you are a professional member of the exchange. At worst the smallest retail traders, submicroscopic ticks on the back of the exchange volume rhinoceros, will pay the bourse fees of barely a dollar or two – significantly less than one basis point. It is to the eternal credit of exchanges that they have mastered the fine art of transacting huge volumes at incredibly low costs that allow wholesale and retail customers alike to enjoy ever lower commissions. Try this with a banker. Where exchange economics are secured by modern micropayments, bankers are still broadly rooted in charging basis points i.e. 0.01 per cent (and usually generous multiples thereof) if not full percentage points.

Moreover, most exchanges, at least the largest and most successful amongst them, have realised the core principle of networked technology: commoditization drives tiny levels of fee charge per transaction and such micropayments are the future of most electronic commerce.

Meanwhile, it would be very easy to simply discuss a narrative of the world moving from an established west towards a dynamic east – but then this book would be getting ahead of itself before our story has barely begun. Moreover, the process is not remotely so simple as to be discerned as universally orientally monodirectional. Indeed, the origins of the whole concept of the microfinancial world have their origins physically in eastern territory. Yet micropayment concepts are now migrating west with vigour. However, whereas originally a lumpen mass of cheap labour seeking a vast improvement in living standards was the catalyst for microbanking to develop under pioneers such as Muhammad Yunus, the western equivalent is entirely as a result of the deployment of technology delivering incremental, as opposed to more radical, change in living standards. Perhaps most excitingly that technology is now also being deployed with devastating effect in the eastern, and particularly the world's emerging markets, too to better scale the original human-centric microfinance models.

Moreover, it would be hugely simplistic to observe merely a 'great leap forward' to China and the east. Rather a broad number of, often disparate, regions are now advancing. Even allowing for not all to maintain the journey, several regions will grow significantly both parallel to western economic recovery and in their own right, relative to the traditionally prosperous west. How the west reacts perhaps is more in the hands of those who believe in inevitable western decline or those who see growth as an ongoing opportunity for all – this is nevertheless more a political domain issue than a purely financial technology one. At the same time, the one area where politics is key is in the generation of trust – those regimes which lose trust, lose prosperity. Those which have our trust gain assets as well as accumulating wealth for their citizens as, for instance, the continuing rise of the City state of Singapore exemplifies.

Stepping back to look at the ongoing revolution, if this sounds like a degree of orderly chaos, then you are clearly mirroring my own thoughts. Revolutions are rarely linear nor do they involve equivalent baby steps. Rather some things advance by leaps and bounds. Meanwhile in other areas, entrenched vested interests fight often savage rearguard actions to protect their privileges and position. As things stand, the fabric of commerce has never been more fluid while government appears all too often to simply seek to tax and impede trade flows.

There is a worrying macro at the time of writing, that many governments appear to share a paucity of ability to engender hope in their economic management ability. This impacts fintech and trading markets more significantly than appears widely recognised. An element of government support is helpful as is the engendering of trust across the economy. I have witnessed at first hand the failure of free investment markets to be broadly accepted through various emerging market lenses – perhaps most notably when I ran an integrated stock and derivatives exchange in Romania. There, trust in transactions was very low and trust in government at an equivalently low level. Moreover, the issue of government support for market structure is not about subsidies or direct payments but rather coherent government engagement to maximize the benefit of markets for all citizens... Indeed in a digital age markets are more open to broad citizen participation, provided regulators are not overly zealous in their exclusions. This only makes it all the more disappointing when governments do not actively support in thought, word and deed their stock exchanges as agents of economic growth and investment returns.

Despite everything that has occurred in the past 20 years one thing has remained the same: the remarkable eco-systems that frame the financial markets of the United States and the United Kingdom. These nations house the world's largest international financial centres, some way ahead of their fast growing Asian competitors and light years ahead of anything continental Europe can muster, despite all manner of efforts to capture business within the EU27 post Brexit.

In the case of the City of London, there is absolutely no doubt that the City is well placed to flourish, even in spite of government which has serially failed to support the City sufficiently in recent times (within certain areas recent regimes have verged on outright hostility towards financial markets despite claiming some vestige of free market hue). The rest of this book will mellifluously seek to sidestep the Brexit situation where the British government has spent years in uncomprehending paralysis at the idea the general public might not see the EU as the success the Brussels machine ascribes to itself. Thankfully that seems to be changing as this book goes to press and indeed I am hugely optimistic that Britain can thrive...As this book has gone through its final draft there appears to have been a genuine outbreak of government for the first time in a decade or more and Brexit will occur soon after this book is published.

The City of London has such a critical mass in expertise and capital that, presuming the government sees some vague vestige of sense and eschews immature populist responses on taxation and regulatory issues, there is an outstanding future for Britain's international financial centre in a truly cosmopolitan nation which prides itself on centuries of international trading relations dating back to long before the term 'globalisation' had ever even been considered. That said the strength which could be found if the UK government coherently regains/maintains a faith in markets and liberty would be more astounding still.

As the epicentre of the US marketplace, the financial centre of New York, and those in the regions of the US are unlikely to see their status dissolve either. At the same time, there is little question that these financial centres will see their position reduced as a proportion of global financial business due to the rise of various eastern centres. However, the concept that Hong Kong, Mumbai (or the currently designated IFSC: GIFT City), Shanghai or Singapore will take over from London or New York as the pre-eminent centres is highly premature. Presuming that is, the governments do not completely abrogate any ability for even a vague vestige of coherent fiscal thought. (Tragically for those of us who have lived through the ongoing Euro crisis of recent years, this is not entirely impossible...). Nevertheless the major financial centres, even while they may see a reduction in their proportion of business, it will be as the pie grows and delivers prosperity to all who continue to engage with the Capital Market Revolution! process.

When it comes to the US dollar, the epitaphs have already been written in many quarters but actually the death of the dollar is, probably, a long way off. The dollar will continue to be the major currency in the world albeit with a likely declining overall share of global reserves. Cryptocurrencies will rise to participate in the share of reserves in due course. The 'tail' currencies such as Japan/UK/ Canada and so forth will likely retain their minor rankings but it is clear that if one (or several) major emerging nations can coherently grow their monetary system and become truly interoperable and develop robust freely floating currencies then it stands to reason that their 'fiat' will gain market share as a proportion of global reserves. What happens to the Euro ought to be the subject of a separate analysis beyond the scope of this book. However, at the time of writing the complete disregard for coherent economics demonstrated over several long years of fiscal ineptitude amongst the Eurozone suggests the European single currency's fate will be a very binary shock after which it will probably entirely cease to exist, or ends up as a Germano-Benelux rump, once fiscally incontinent nations elsewhere find it impossible to remain part of this tragically flawed experiment. That is not a fintech observation, merely common sense, Victory would appear unlikely for the Euro, Death is hardly implausible even if it is a fairly seismic moment which will redefine the European project (and again that probably doesn't look like it can claim much of a coherent victory over anything in the short term either...).

The man who deployed the term "Victory or Death" Rudolf Ferscha subsequently moved effortlessly to the global financial centre of London and into venture capital where he has maintained a strong investing track record. However in 2002 he hit the nail on the head with his hyper-prescient remarks about the future outlook for exchanges. Those remarks stand true today for anybody engaged in economic activity across the world – particularly in financial markets.

If you are a fresh faced millennial convinced of the wonders of cooperation at every stage, I seek not to destroy every vestige of your belief. I too firmly want you to succeed, for the pie to grow and indeed to attain a "win win" situation. However we need to be more than a bullshit bingo card of aphorisms and there needs to be a cold hard worldview, as Rudi famously espoused. Understand that cooperation is one thing but the cold light of day always reveals a competitive urge / survival instinct nexus at which point proper free markets exist and deliver better lives and more prosperity for everybody. In that sense, this is no hipster treatise on the wonders of how banks cooperate with fintech – far from it. It is, as Capital Market

Revolution! was before it, a cold hard light of day examination of the physics of markets having a chemical reaction with the biology of technology.

In this book, I want to cut through and help promote better understanding of some key precepts in the fintech world right now, why they matter and what their legacy impact will likely prove. It's a response to a series of questions I have been hearing repeatedly over the years.

As an investor and trader in my own right, I have always lived by the maxim 'roughly right is better than completely wrong.' If you wonder what qualifies me to deliver my insights in the world of fintech, please bear in mind that when it came to the Capital Market Revolution! I was way beyond 'roughly right' with my predictions. Indeed I turned out to be more accurate than I had ever anticipated.

Ladies and gentlemen, however you view the Capital Market Revolution! to date... no matter how you perceive the future of financial technology and its interaction with society and the global economy from the macro to the micro... there is no third way: the simple binary question which affects us at the heart of the debate remains "Victory or Death?"

As you're reading this book, I presume you aren't doing so out of a masochistic desire to fail.

"New technology is common, new thinking is rare."
Sir Peter Blake

Prologue - Where The One-Eyed Man Is King

Apu: "I enrolled at Springfield Heights Institute of Technology under the tutelage of the brilliant professor, John Frink."

Professor John Frink: "Well, sure, the Frinkiac 7 looks impressive – don't touch it – but I predict that within 100 years, computers will be twice as powerful and so expensive that only the five richest kings of Europe will own them."[1]

Where Capital Market Revolution! was a breathless look at the future – this tome is somewhat different. Yes, the perspective is still progressive but in many ways it is a survival manual of sorts for anybody who is trying to get their head around just what is the perspective on trends and technologies within the fintech ambit. It is a direct response to countless (in the thousands) of similar questions I have been asked over the years.

Reading the book: while it can flow as a narrative of sorts, it is also intended to be broadly modular. I wrote it to be easily readable from start to finish. However, at the same time you are welcome to delve in wherever you wish. Each chapter retains its own characteristics and essentially functions as a standalone essay. At the same time, forgive me if therefore I indulge in a little delicate repetition every so often to enable this variety of reading approaches. Anyway, fret not, the 'plot' won't become opaque if you don't do a linear read through progressing from page 1 to touching the Z's in the index. If you do

1. "The Simpsons" Series 7 Episode 23 "Much Apu About Nothing"

read from start to finish you may be a little delayed by some lightly repetitive explanations.

However, while you are here... in order to find a decent starting point, let's take a step back to the last millennium AKA twenty years ago. In those days when folks were championing the World Wide Web as the "Information Superhighway" it was fascinating as a financial practitioner and digital pioneer to see the incredible change taking place, often rapidly. At the same time I had a front row seat to observe the remarkable stench of self-important stasis broadly maintained throughout the financial industry from the wholesale all the way through retail 'services.' After a number of years of championing the financial marketplace online from the interweb itself – as you have gathered already – my first book "Capital Market Revolution!" was published by FT Prentice Hall on July 1st 1999.

Looking back from the current era of smartphone enabled drone-laden, social media centric digital ubiquity a couple of decades later "CMR!" may strike many like an odd period piece. The biggest thing youthful innovators will ask incredulously is "but wasn't it all obvious?"

To which the answer, I can assure you all, remains: "Not remotely!" Or at least not remotely to many... At this time the band of folks who were pioneering the ranks of what has subsequently become a global fintech movement of millions, were few and far between. Moreover, we pioneers were in varying measures regarded with a mixture of fear, loathing and terror by most institutions. In fact those recalcitrant emotions applied only to the more innovative for profit entities. The NGO's and government bodies evoked a broad measure of 100% absolutist pure play denial. Regulators had a curious tendency to stroke huge swathes of papers straddling their in-tray when presented with the eventuality of a digital future. This paperwork carressing provided them with a sense of calm cum security blanket as I tried to explain just why everything was about to change. Needless to say the message about what they needed to do to position themselves to avoid being an impediment to the paradigm shifts, tended to fall on deaf ears.

I know, I know, even then the much used phrase (guilty as charged) "paradigm shift" sounded a bit Davos-vapid. However, I am trying to give a flavour of the breathless excitement which I incessantly exuded. All the while the concepts of fintech were being frequently ignored by folk who sincerely hoped Sisyphus might squash me with that rock of frustration if I chanced to wander past his slope. Indeed the late 1990's marked an era when every regulator appeared to have their own Sisyphean slope just across the hallway from whatever office you happened to be visiting. Nowadays that space seems to be taken up with some form of fintech 'sandbox' – a slightly perplexing term for projects the regulators still can't get their heads around even 20 years after they found themselves fulsomely ignoring the digital world's fintech birth.

Then again looking back to those dizzy pioneering days one can also say of the financial structure / firmament: "plus ça change plus c'est la même chose." This remains a painfully accurate remark almost 2 centuries after the epigram was written by Jean-Baptiste Alphonse Karr in his (January 1849) satirical journal Les Guêpes. The banking industry remains a key pivotal part of the financial infrastructure and the major players in most every aspect of extant pre-digital financial activity are predominantly legacy financial players. That said, there are some upstarts who have already become world leaders. Think of Intercontinental Exchange which has, in barely 20 years gone from a niche turnaround play to become a leading element of the exchange establishment. In the late 1990's ICE amounted to a rescued power business seeking an energy market platform pivot which had been bought for a single dollar in 1997. Nowadays ICE is conspicuously the single largest exchange winner from the Capital Market Revolution! having grown its value from negative (that dollar purchase price included a swathe of liabilities) to one of the world's leading exchange groups, worth in excess of 50 billion dollars.

Despite the incumbent regulatory privileges of many financial market participants, the world of fintech is delivering revolutionary process to the financial marketplace faster than ever. True, average fintech folk will gush all about the delights of cooperation with existing incumbents and the like... However, having weathered the revolution this far, I come from more cynical stock. The gushy millennial happy cooperative stuff – call me cynical or realistic – strikes me as little short of imbecilic. This remains full contact capitalism for scarce financial assets and valuable customers. Cooperation is just supplicancy serving better coffee beans to induce a false sense of security. I reserve the right to change my opinion as the facts change. Moreover, I am a huge optimist. Nevertheless, I prefer my optimism tinged with realism. Realpolitik too. The way I see it, a lot of tired old linear entities with a focus on pure survival whose practitioners intend to exercise their maximum pension rights, are tending to operate something tantamount to corporate paedophilia with a naive backbone of millenials.[2] I do think it is fair to wonder just what happens when the massive plays on audience size (which can tend towards the painfully customer oblivious) run out of their copious unicorn reserves of funding? If that happens in a downturn, the banks more than likely will have (once again) run out of money too. Food for thought. Or sleepless nights if you are a classic 'me too' genre VC/PE player.

Anyway, I tend to see the future of markets as one which results in direct competition overcoming the limits of the legacy regulatory monopolies behind which all too many incumbents are cowering in the hope of surviving what has until now been a relatively light siege. The existing entities predating the latest innovations ostensibly seek

2. I appreciate this may be a strong statement for some but it is merely the next generation successor to my noting that "marrying your cousins does not neccessarily improve the quality of the gene pool" concerning cross-town stock and futures exchange mergers during the 1990's.

to maintain the Churchillian maxim to "Keep Buggering On." Hence I see the resolution as a true binary emerging from Schumpeterian "Creative Destruction:" Victory or Death! Schumpeterian process is something politicians tend tend to resist at all costs with all manner of interventions until they run out of fingers to plug the multiplying holes in the dam. Having deployed all their dam-plugging digits it is not long before the flood waters overcome the incumbents. In that sense, financial innovation remains a game of 'elephant and mouse.' Here the massive banking pachyderms crowd out everyone else in the room while maintaining an attention seeking "me me me" mentality. This is liberally laced with some Stockholm syndrome moves on the government-regulatory blob. The end result tends to be paralysis of the establishment, or, at worst, bailing out of banks on a 'payment for failure' basis. Thus if you are a large enough financial player, you receive similar rules to the often conspicuous consumption meets opaque losses of the government sector. "Heads I win, tails you bail me out" banking will I suspect reach a conspicuous denouement in a recession coming to our economies soon. Unsurprisingly it seems the general public would prefer efficiency and indeed accountability on the occasion of failure.

It is worth going back to the original "Capital Market Revolution!" and noting how some of the premises contained therein have played out since 1998 when the book was written. Remember that at the time many were viewed with little short of dripping contempt by the legacy entities. Musings that the Chicago Board of Trade would not long survive as an indepdendent entity if it didn't change its operations were regarded as idiotic.

The CBOT was acquired by CME within 7 years of CMR! being published.

Equally some delicious anomalies have arisen. The 'ultras' such as myself saw no future for floor trading while the reactionaries were convinced they could broadly survive. Within a year or two of Capital Market Revolution! being published it was increasingly obvious to all and sundry – well apart from some staff at the likes of CBOE and other slow moving bourses – that floor trading was dead and electronic trading marked the way forward. Barely a few floors are still in existence. The only one which appears to retain a viable business case is the London Metals Exchange, part of the Hong Kong Exchanges leviathan. The LME, now at the northern end of the Square Mile, works because it has proven cost effective at delivering a stream of focussed price 'fixings,' all from a rather compact 4000 square foot 'ring.' This last floor in the City of London is repurposed for every 15 minute fixing session. By comparison the last London interest rate through to stock index futures hybrid floor at LIFFE which closed on November 24, 2000, comprised thousands of floors traders across 40,000 square feet of high ceilinged (aka multi storey) premium office space above Cannon Street station. The dealing pattern there of continuous markets required separate pits open throughout the day thus delivering a huge cost in people and infrastructure as each pit had separate staff – both from the broker / dealer side as well as the exchange operator itself. Essentially the same LME staff and market participants make the deals every fixing session across a range of metals.

Across the Atlantic, the historic floor of the New York Stock Exchange has been retained, albeit it strikes me more as a media showpiece for the opening and closing bell ceremonies with an element of dealing taking place through human interaction. 24 hour rolling cable stations have deemed that the televisual impact of markets involves many human bodies. At the same time there is a fascinating proxy war waging for the future of media from the same iconic Wall Street building. In that sense is the future of investing television CNBC or Chedr? (I tend to increasingly believe in the latter digital 'dairy' hegemony albeit that too is under constant pressure as the cost to market of narrow/broadcasting delivers a very different segmenting of the media from the delightful old notion that living room corners needed a big boxy screen tube contraption). For all the talk of markets having an epicentre in Wall Street, in reality the material execution of stock market business nowadays is to be found throbbing through servers in places like Mahwah New Jersey. There the data centres of the major exchanges and market platforms are surrounded by the low latency boxes laden with the algorithms of High Frequency Traders (HFT). A vast cornucopia of traders and investors then connect to the marketplace via their own dedicated networks and the internet. Where telephony was driving orders in the 1980s and 1990s, nowadays voice connected traders are a paucity of order flow. Meanwhile Mahwah New Jersey is a truly virtual financial centre. Indeed Mahwah amounts to the biggest financial centre in history no financial practitioners have ever visited.

Therein the CMR! thesis of networked digital technology has held up resolutely. Electronic markets have enabled volumes to grow vastly beyond levels at which floor markets could reasonably cope. While volume grew exponentially, the only foible in the CMR! canon was to suggest that bandwidth growth would be able to keep up. My bad. This prediction has proven to be completely false. Seeking to restrict bandwidth usage, exchanges and markets have over the years partaken in more modes of "throttling" than those 50 shades of fictional bondage characters Christian Grey and Anastasia Steele. My CMR! era optimism has since been tempered with the realisation that the growth in human ingenuity to deploy bandwidth grows at an exponentially faster rate than cables or wireless (or even infrared) networks can be established or expanded. Given that relentless expansion of network capacity during the past 20 years, it also has to be said financial market users have been assiduous in their essentially insatiable desire to use more data than can be supplied by the prevailing technology.

In many ways I didn't anticipate predicting anything with "Capital Market Revolution!" I just intended to write a book showing that the old ways were reaching the end of their useful life and how it was feasible to draw linear progressions to a digital future in markets, investment products, intermediaries, financial centres, funds, forex et al. Somewhere along the line I became one of the people who helped create what are nowadays called prediction markets (the concept was mentioned in CMR! just as industry leader Betfair was being coded in secret). I was an early advocate for sports and political trading via exchanges which led to my becoming a co-founder of Tradesports/Intrade. In due course the name "prediction markets" was adopted for this segment which I must admit has always confused me as this surely infers that other markets are non-predictive? Now, if other markets are not predicting then it means their pricing is inherently understood and ergo it must be possible to know what price the market will be – which in and of itself is entirely untrue about any free market I have ever seen… Anyway, the name prediction markets has stuck, even if it is somewhat of an oxymoron. Somewhere along the line I played a modest role in their genesis.

At the same time, in my line of work as an analyst turned trader, I used an often vivid imagination to develop all manner of scenarios. Perhaps being an early adopter of computers helped too. My first PC, a Sinclair ZX81 hummed with the promise of the future particularly when that apparently colossal at the time 16K expansion RAM pack was added to its 8K ROM and 1K initial RAM. Or maybe that brief exposure to the delights of the classics – Latin and Ancient Greek have actually proven more useful in the development of my thought process than any other avenue I studied…

Whatever it was, the simple truth is I happened to see a lot of things developing along the tracks and having been an early adopter of screen-based trading (albeit still entering orders by phone in the early stages), I appreciated by the mid-1990s that the world of markets was about to undergo enormous change – a greater change than had ever taken place before…

….At which point the narrative could have easily ground to a halt. Efforts to launch a fund to take advantage of the brave new world of fintech didn't even achieve an apathetic response, it was a profound disdain of the sort which might have been justified for the many charlatans espousing alchemy in the 12th century. In essence, nobody seemed to want to know about fintech in 1995/6.

Then I went travelling. Nowadays there is a movement of 'digital nomads' who set down their rucksacks and whip out their MacBook in far away places. Pausing only to affect a quick combing of hair to look casually fabulous for their Instagram feed, they identify the local wifi code and live the dream of being perpetual travellers with a digital ability to work from anywhere they choose. Back in the mid 1990's I did the same thing. Lurking in an attic, is a separate duffel bag I had to haul around replete with all manner of plastic doohickeys and dongles, endless types of cables and a multitude of sockets, screwdrivers et al. This component kit enabled what passed for effortless (sic) digital nomadry (via dial up) back in the days when the internet was a rare thing to behold and connecting to it involved skills that were not far short of the digital equivalent of water divining.

Even from the position of far from 'plug and play' nomadry, it wasn't difficult to see the world was going to change. well, at least in terms of financial structure, I didn't envisage Facebook or Instagram so clearly I didn't have a holistic answer! However, in the realm of finance, it was not hard to see how, whether from northern winter avoidance spaces across Australia and south-east Asia, or summer haunts around Italy and the Mediterranean... that the world of finance was set for profound change.

Think of it – lots of folks waving their arms at each other and shouting orders which were written on pieces of paper and then tossed into the arms of the waiting 'runners' or sometimes just dropped on the floor for them to collect. (I am nowadays always reminded of a busy floor trading day in the aftermath of the ticker tape parades which accompany the procession of statues of saints through the streets of my adopted hometown Valletta during local religious festivals). No real time understanding of what people's net positions were, other than their own handwritten records... A paucity of information on the quality of trade execution (timestamps occured when bits of papers transgressed a booth and that was about it)... in other words a hugely complex series of human interactions worked remarkably efficiently. However it was at risk of enabling all known foibles of humanity and it bore the peril of human borne errors. In efficiency terms old fashioned markets were invariably slowed by the natural human need to eat, sleep and perform other bodily functions.

I realised this all had to change. The more I travelled the more I realised it didn't matter whether I said so or not, the change was inevitable. However, there was a niche opening to predict the future. When I appreciated the tipping point of floor trading having been surpassed by the then cutting edge – AKA what is nowadays hyper-rudimentary – technology, it seemed like an idea to try to redouble my efforts to see who might listen to the concept of change in financial markets.

I published a lot online. Some read, some paid attention, most didn't... Then when the opportunity fortuitously arose, I doubled down and wrote a book.

Looking back on that tome 20 years on, I suppose the best compliment anybody paid was a young chap of the modern fintech genus. You would doubtless recognise the hipster millennial types to whom I refer. Confident, outgoing, amiable, convinced of their own innate brilliance and yet, oddly lacking in perspective, particularly to the dark ages. Oh and by dark ages, I mean pretty much anytime before the internet arrived. To the hipster 'fintecher,' people who used desktop boxes chipped with 386s (the Intel 80386 series) were savage barbarians in mud huts. Given my ZX81 being followed by the Sinclair Spectrum, then an Amstrad PCW 8256...In many of their eyes, I remain a genuine cave dweller. Anyway when handed a copy of the "Capital Market Revolution!" this millennial came away intrigued. This was a few years ago when the notion of reading was apparently only to be undertaken on a Kindle or tablet computer. Thus the notion that the origins of fintech were recorded in a 'book' – that bizarrely analogue mashing of trees into tomes – was, in and of itself, intriguing.

Fair enough, 'book' is an odd interface to look at. While the GUI can be changed it involves a lot of recycling and the weight is a fascinating insight into what trees can deliver. Anyway, this fintech youth read "Capital Market Revolution!" and delivered the fascinating insight: "But this is all obvious!"

I probably laughed a little too maniacally. Unlike the 'blood on the streets' genre of political revolution, I hadn't felt fear during the Capital Market Revolution! Albeit, there were a few, well, motivating and life affirming moments... There were times in front of some floor traders who rather cherished their jobs and resented anybody suggesting their impending redundancy. Craning my neck to the lofty heights of the more accomplished pit brokers made me acutely aware that they didn't have a healthy regard for people who were trying – no matter how politely – to explain that their livelihood was endangered by technology. Managerial cadres have never whipped out thumb screws but I suspect they secretly wanted to... They have indulged in the most fascinating of passive aggressive if not merely outright 'aggressive aggressive' dynamics to convince me that there was a reason why a human on the end of a computer could do a better job executing orders than a network cable between two computers being left to get on with a little 'SCSI chat.' Indeed in one memorable instance, I was summarily removed from the floor of the then epicentre of oil trading, the New York Mercantile Exchange. Apparently I was fomenting revolution in the eyes of the official concerned.

...In essence, having seen the frontline of the revolution, I can still clearly recall just how completely and utterly NOT REMOTELY obvious the march of digital technology in financial markets was to most prevailing practitioners 20 years ago.

That said, there is no argument for taking the track record of "Capital Market Revolution!" and ascribing too much to its legacy. Nevertheless many vestiges of the tome worked out as broadly predicted. That many trends remain relevant 20 years on continues to pleasantly surprise me to this day. It can be attributed to a delightful nexus of inspiration, perspiration, good timing and that frequently essential element to human achievement at the right moment in the right place, a dollop of good luck.

However, having been one of the relatively few folks in the asylum of markets willing to suggest major change was afoot...and after another couple of decades with a rather not too shabby record of maintaining such prognoses somewhat accurately, I do feel it is only fair to note that the very words I live by when making these predictions is a wonderful proverb which my good friend Bob Paul pointed out to me some years ago and has repeated often since:

"In the land of the blind, the one-eyed man is king."

Or as I once remarked – and as has since become somewhat of a stock in trade remark on a heap of online quotation directories:

"The trouble with weather forecasting is that it's right too often for us to ignore it and wrong too often for us to rely on it."

The latter has been broadly circulating in its own parallel existence over the years alongside my fintech theses. I suppose the remark hits the spot at the epicentre of human life that can be appreciated by all citizens of the world, on a much broader subject matter than looking at injecting new ways of thinking, working and deploying technology in finance. This book does not deal with meteorology but it does look at the future of finance. However you deem it, perhaps this metaphorically one eyed man can again show you some areas where there is much to be thought about the future of finance and the future of markets.

My one concern however remains as follows: While weather shapes our lives and everybody talks about it, money shapes our lives just as much (if not more) on an everyday basis. Yet many people are not eager to understand it. Nor are many others eager to seek to improve how finance works.

Therefore, with one clear eye on the future I have written this tome in the interest of spreading understanding, enrishing more people with knowledge that can deliver a broader prosperity.

Introduction

"Day two is stasis followed by irrelevance followed by excruciatingly painful decline followed by death and that is why it is always day one."

Jeff "It's always day one at Amazon" Bezos

Welcome to another Day One in Fintech. The hour has come to advance the Capital Market Revolution! once more. If you're in day two, you must be part of legacy finance... Day one dawns as it has for so many days since 1999 (and before) when the revolution was born. Day one looks even more complex now, a different digital world, one where the pace of change is, if anything, accelerating. Even those blessed with legacy regulatory privilege are feeling the heat.

"Victory or Death?" is not another volume of blistering futurespeak but it is unrepentantly a tome devoted to our digital future in finance. However this is in many ways a chance to reset yourself to day one – today's day one – to better break down and appreciate some of the key dynamics in modern financial technology and how they are changing the world.

Whether you are absolutely new to the world of fintech or you have been involved with finance for years, then this book is for you. Indeed, if you aren't involved with finance in any way...then I am minded to wonder how you managed to successfully buy this book? Indeed are the shelves in your mud hut good for storing books in paper or digital format? #Srsly: Unless you are living off grid, you are involved with finance. Being involved in finance means technology is increasingly playing a role in your financial life. In many ways that all began over 20 years ago when I termed the phrase "Capital Market Revolution!" to describe the seismic impact of networked technology reshaping every vestige of organised markets... From there what became known as fintech has infiltrated every strand of financial activity.

In 1999 most markets still traded through "open outcry" – with folks shouting at each other and writing orders on cards to be manually processed by back office staff in booths on the floor. "CMR!" set the tone for what was certainly a revolution. That journey ranged from predicting prediction markets to explaining the future of products, all the way through to outlining the bright future for electronic money (some nowadays might notice a resemblance to cryptocurrency). It was a tale of how a raft of new products would be commonplace for trading, such as electricity and emissions while at the centrepiece of many investor portfolios would sit Exchange Traded Funds (ETFs).

Thereafter I wasn't merely a passive observer spotting the future trend of financial technology. I helped develop and popularise Single Stock Futures to spread across the world – to what was initially widespread scepticism. I co-founded the prediction market GSX/Tradesports/Intrade and did a lot of work with multiple leading exchanges, from helping the CME transition their traders "from Floor To Screen," to introducing EUREX to DTCC (which led to a later investment). That was just one of several deals, while I also chaired the leading conference on financial centres, and even ran a small vertically integrated exchange group.

Given that I wrote the first book of fintech which is now 20 years old, you have clearly deduced I am not a millennial. Rather I come from Generation BALD. Perhaps I am a charter member but the, er, bald, truth is, I at least (self-)defined the acronym. For all those obsessed with X'ers, millennials et al, G-BALD is just another variation on a theme albeit this one is defined by technology. I realised the differential when dealing with the so-called 'digital natives' AKA those born sometime in the Millennial or Generation Z brackets (essentially from the 1980s on: albeit I really think digital natives were only holistically minted after the internet was widely developed – which means at the earliest the mid 1990's and realistically 2000 AD).

If your birth took place before the turn of the millennium you effectively retain some element of BALD DNA. As you may have gathered this has nothing to do with the notion of hairline. The acronym stands for "Born Analogue, Lives Digital." Indeed you may have been born quite some time before 2000 A.D. My good friend and fellow tech/fintech pioneer Colin Howard is amongst those most deserving of this moniker. He is enjoying what some might call the 'third age' with admirable aplomb as a vigorous septuagenarian. However, BALD he most certainly is! Being BALD, age is irrelevant but attitude is essential: the key qualifying factor is that you "Live Digital." That disqualifies the vast majority of folk in any age group. Merely using or engaging actively with technology is insufficient. Being truly BALD means Living Tech, as in encountering tech like a native, even if it has been a process of assimilation unlike that of the generation born with a silver iPad in their mouths.

Some -ologists deploy a phrase "digital immigrant." I find this rather unedifying as it suggests people born before the digital age don't belong in the future. Nobody deserves to be held in a virtual holding centre of digital doubt awaiting processing even if they are 100% analogue. Moreover being a digital immigrant doesn't infer the holistic nature of actually embracing the 'tech thing.' The Living Digital element makes the BALD stand out in many ways. Indeed digital immigrants may not live tech, they may merely be cybersquatting for convenience. On the contrary, the BALD generation do: they have assimilated their native attitude in a fashion akin to those delicious folks who may be more English than the English, despite having been born far far away in terms of geography and nationality.

When it comes to being BALD, our generation got into tech when it was a lot more 'hands on' than it is today. Our first computing devices did pretty much that – compute – with few frills. We may have built the machine ourselves in whole or part and we almost certainly had to know how to boot an OS to see signs of interaction with the rather massive screens prevalent in an era before the human to GUI device slimmed down below size 0 thickness. Some of these early microcomputers required a television to plug in to (I won't bore with you analogue anecdotes, you can Google / Duck Duck search 'television' if you're from the Youtube generation). This pioneering constructionist approach towards our first computers may not seem a massive advantage in the modern day where anything which takes longer than 30 seconds to 'plug and play' is regarded as hard labour by the digitally native generation. However our more 'hands on' assemblage roots do serve to give us a certain understanding of computer construction which is beyond that of those who merely *use* technology. BALD folk may be barely able to program, or they may have learnt what are classical languages of coding like Cobol or Basic. Just as some folks with even a vague old school smattering of Ancient Greek or Latin can be wildly effective in the modern world (that's my story and I'm sticking to it) so too the programmers of the classical codes have an intuition for everything digital even if they struggle to discern Python at first glance, or would be derailed by Ruby.

In addition to being BALD when it comes to technology, in many ways I am an atypical financial professional. For one thing I like people to understand investment and finance. It never ceases to appall me that there is a veil of opacity across much of the financial world placed there by practitioners who suggest the fiscal world is so complex most normal folks will struggle to comprehend it.

This has always struck me as a lousy argument. A defeatist dogma which undermines delivering a financial "win win." When lying in a hospital bed awaiting an operation, no matter how trivial or complex, recall the bedside manner of the surgeon and anaesthetist. How do you expect them to enquire about the conduct of the upcoming medical procedure? If either party looked at you and replied – as a financier habitually does in their own field – that this is a complex procedure and hence they cannot explain what will happen in surgery... as you snooze away thanks to a heady cocktail of drugs administered by an expert who will keep you alive but asleep and bereft of pain at the point of incision.

...Well, faced with a financial-style sandbagging explanation from the physicians, I believe most of us would be endeavouring to exit the hospital post haste, ripping the intravenous drip from our arms as we hastened to grab our clothes and rapidly escape the surgeon's clutches of opaque non-explanation.

Of course the hospital reality is this: Unlike 'it's complicated!' financial folk, rather the doctors go out of their way to explain in hugely simple, if not downright simplistic terms, what they are going to do. "A little nick here and I will have you as right as rain..." is a decent paraphrase. Nobody for a moment – least of all the patient – thinks surgery is that easy but it is a process of confidence building and a courtesy which helps patients maintain their faith in those excellent professionals bound by the Hippocratic oath.

Alas the financial industry struggles with radiating comprehension and courtesy. Indeed the arrival of millennial fintech folk making fintech waves in places hasn't overly improved the gene pool when it comes to making finance more accessible. More available – yes. More accessible and comprehensible... actually not. To some extent this may continue to blunt the impact of fintech: The financial industry needs to stop commingling confusion and contempt towards customers. Thus fintech too must get its act together with some genuine customer service fit for the digital age. Without that, fintech and finance will struggle to deliver the trust to establish any form of cohesive financial intermediation.

True, the political – regulatory blob doesn't help either when it comes to improving financial literacy. Nor has it overly coherently encouraged the financial industry to genuinely engage in transparency. Regulation has veered too close to becoming a perverse act of determination to avoid risk to the point where consumers are broadly infantilized...and vast risks emerge because the customers have been prevented from taking control of their finances. Worse still, too many consumers seem to wallow in the power of their own thoughts being taken away from them... With our digital world of Wiki-stuff, let alone a million podcasts and online videos explaining just about everything (albeit to varying standards of probity / accuracy and comprehensivity), it is odd that the blob still sees investment as something everybody must be protected from as opposed to encouraging folks towards greater financial literacy. It is a remarkable irony that despite being the best ever system for distributing knowledge, the digital world attracts yet more regulation when 'the truth is out there' readily accessible across the ether. At this point, it is fair to say that of the two things "Capital Market Revolution!" got wrong in 1999, one was the ongoing extensive crawl of regulation into all manner of digital crevices. (The other: that market connectivity bandwidth would expand more rapidly than investors/traders could deploy it – quite the contrary! Human ingenuity can eat bandwidth faster than anybody can deliver it!).

When it comes to regulation and fintech, this conversation could rapidly devolve into a discussion on how things have of late become so bizarre that processes which must cost money are at the time of writing being allowed by regulators to be marketed as 'free.' In essence if something creates friction, something somewhere is being deployed to pay for the energy of that friction... Anyone with a scintilla of common sense can see that 'free' here is a synonym for 'costs buried within the product.' This is of course odd and contradictory. For digital 'millennial-friendly' product in stock trading is essentially implicitly laden with hidden costs while regulators are viciously endeavouring (and quite rightly too) to have total cost / commission transparency in traditional financial markets. Readers may wish to consider whether this is as a result of regulators being far from BALD but rather purely analogue...or simply hypocritical.

Nevertheless, despite there being a vogue for infantilization, opacity and a paucity of explanation from much of the financial mainstream (old tech or new…), I have spent the past 20 years and more trying to break down into explicable bite sized chunks the significance of particular issues / thoughts and processes. Indeed that is where "Victory or Death?" fits into the jigsaw of comprehension.

Right now in the world of fintech it would be glib to merely dismiss progress as #Itscomplicated. However, clearly a lot is going on and a great deal of process is being developed – often very rapidly – which is changing the way networks interact and thus people can invest / manage their money and indeed pay their bills etc.

The title "Victory or Death?" is intended to focus the mind. Some might see it as a touch passive aggressive. However, it is the simple binary of outcomes ahead. Understand this stuff or face the reduction of your income, perhaps the end of your career. On an investment level, the risks are not merely a loss in investment ability but the prospect of total investment immolation at the personal portfolio level. Again, my intention is not to trigger you, just to ensure you appreciate what is important here. The processes of fintech are changing lives and we're on the cusp of a great acceleration. I would like you to be on the positive side of that life changing ledger. Given you have made it this far in the narrative already, I suspect you feel the same way.

A quarter of a century ago, I started a conversation about markets through the wondrous new interweb thing. This was back when HTML was pretty much everything a web site could be. Java and CSS were just beginning to come onstream. My pioneering readers preferred the Netscape browser and we didn't Google anything because it wasn't invented until several years later. The online conversation via the WWW led to a life as an early digital nomad taking me around the world, meeting folks in markets across the globe. Driven by my internet epiphany (none at over 28.8K baud I hasten to add), my appreciation of the nature of network power led me to write the first bestselling fintech book. A delightful folio of reprocessed trees greeted the great and the good at the British

Library on July 1st where my publishers FT Prentice Hall showcased the tome and life was never quite the same again.

Capital Market Revolution!

Three simple words everybody in finance needed to understand. The time for digital was upon us.

CMR! had been several years in the making ever since, as I mentioned, I got playing with WWW in 1994. At that time I was already a somewhat pioneering electronic trader with several years trading experience via screens (who had started on the open outcry floors in London).

At the time Capital Market Revolution! was published, the markets were ill prepared. Many exchanges were still sticking – stubbornly / desperately – to their pits – despite what had happened to LIFFE in the face of the DTB Bund juggernaut. (I wrote a first history of the "Battle of the Bund" in CMR!) The outlook for the LIFFE exchange itself remained somewhat touch and go.

…You've got the gist. In 1999, the investment world was on the cusp of upheaval and a lot of folks wondered how the regulatory system would cope. Elsewhere the incumbents were doing everything possible to cover up the brave new world emerging around them and seeking to keep us back in the analogue age. Some cunning reactionaries were adroitly endeavouring to smear a new shade of lipstick on the analogue pig of finance. They maintained a desperate hope markets could stay within an established comfort zone with lots of people, lots of staff and loads of paper.

Once again it is time to consider those three simple words that are shaping the future of finance as it continues to be upended by disintermediating network economics. In an era of millennial zeitgeist we like cooperation, we love profit and we want to see competition. Good Service is a must, as is understanding what happens when you fail.

Where "Capital Market Revolution!" was the line in 1999, the message in 2019 is simple: "Victory or Death?"

This book looks at the future of market and what's at the epicentre of value, how that interacts with a regulatory system not yet able to cope with deregulation and indeed somewhat stifled in places by the power of the blockchain. Don't forget when it comes to cryptocurrency, Capital Market Revolution! made a huge case for electronic alternative currencies in 1999 – AKA what has become Bitcoin, Ethereum et al subsequently (nope I didn't envisage the DLT bit and I am not claiming to be Satoshi). At the same time: stores of value in tokenized form – well CMR! discussed that too...

Victory or Death? aims to look at a series of key issues shaping the markets of tomorrow and how they interact with the future of finance. I have endeavoured to break each down in a simple fashion so you can better appreciate the rudiments of why blockchain and cryptocurrency matter, along with several other key aspects to our future fintech world.

This isn't the end of the Capital Market Revolution! story. "Victory or Death?" offers a glimpse of the future while endeavouring to place in perspective, key elements of what is changing the financial world around us.

Welcome (back) to Day One in fintech.

1. A Child Is Born

"It will therefore be crucial that you see the world anew. That means looking from the outside in to reanalyze much that you have probably taken for granted. This will enable you to come to an understanding. If you fail to transcend conventional thinking at a time when conventional thinking is losing touch with reality, then you will be more likely to fall prey to an epidemic of disorientation that lies ahead. Disorientation breeds mistakes that could threaten your business, your investments and your way of life."

James Dale Davidson and Lord (William) Rees-Mogg[1]

Valletta, Malta, Sunday September 22nd, 2019: As the Blockchain Island[2] takes shape here in Malta, a child is born. That child is going to live to be 130 years old. Their world will be unlike anything we have ever seen before in history. They are being born into an entirely digital world. Their world, which was the realm of science fiction and fantasy when I was a child during the twilight of the last millennium, presents opportunities, threats and challenges like no other era in human history. This is a world of speed and innovation where a tiny competitive advantage, a mere few microseconds, can give you the opportunity to create vast empires. Amidst massive chances to cooperate, locally, across borders and across continents, there remain huge benefits to being ahead of the competition: the diseases which robbed our forefathers of so many children are declining but for those who prevail and profit, the medieval mantra of "Victory or Death?" rings true more than ever before.

1. The Sovereign Individual, 1997.
2. See DLT Malta - Thoughts From The Blockchain Island, DV Books 2019

When this child reaches the age of 18, they will probably never have a driving license because they'll use a driverless car. Indeed they may never even own a car, sharing in a pool or perhaps just relying on casual rentals for every journey – already a fact of everyday life for thousands of drivers and scooter riders in Malta. Perhaps passenger drone travel will become a handy way to head home late of an evening... Certainly autonomous unmanned aerial vehicles will become a vital element of infrastructure for today's baby's adult infrastructure tomorrow: from grocery deliveries to various safety and security applications. Wherever our child looks, whatever they may do, their lives will be surrounded by and dynamically enhanced by, technology. From the pyrotechnics bringing ancient relics to life in the world's great museums to the way our child's recreational affiliations will be divided between conventional games and e-sports linking players across the world. Today's child will be habituated to listening and watching on demand in a way where the whole concept of tv channels and a fixed programme stack will appear as bizarre to the next generation as taking days riding on stagecoaches to travel across a few hundred miles seemed to mine.

More than any generation, this child is born into a world of pure opportunity. Pure unrelenting opportunity at every turn, powered by digital wonderment.

This child will have incredible opportunities through nanotechnology and biotechnology and naturally, the whole world of finance. The way that they deal with their pension going forward, even whether or not they actually use a bank, those are all going to be radically different throughout the course of their lives. It's not just the online experience, it will be the whole means of dealing with finance. For those who deem the modern marketplace complex, the competing range of cash and cryptocurrency will appear dizzying, let alone the choice of investment product: thousands of options all available for semi-instantaneous settlement. This isn't just about the pure technology facing the child, this is also a derivatives world. The child who thinks in three dimensions financially will be at a huge advantage to those who are limited to the old analogue stock buyers' binary of owning or not owning a share or bond...

Of course, that share has generally become extinct in terms of physical paper trail. Nowadays the trail is digital data. Shares, bonds or other assets are already registered as database entries, entirely 'dematerialised' in the securities industry parlance. However, our child of the future will be wedded to their digital device (next...next...next...next X10 to the power of next...-gen smartphone) which is at once their wallet, their asset manager, bank manager and life coach. The smart device (perhaps linked physically to their body, quite feasibly running a few chips under the skin to make it easier to pass through office security and pay for a coffee via an AI barrista, occasionally even the odd human one) will be the epicentre of their investments, security, calendar and indeed whole life...

...A whole life which today's baby will see as not merely a longer lived one but an exercize in generating and deploying data. Every person born today will create more data in bits and bytes from their very being than was the sum total of accumulated stored human knowledge before 2000 A.D. Already the data footprint of our newborn is growing by the second (even ignoring the repository stored antenatally as they were scanned, screened and examined by all manner of digital devices during those womb-bound months). Now their life functions are being monitored by the second (or less). As they grow, they will be used to monitoring their health, wealth and indeed happiness, in real time. Wherever they go their digital data footprint will leave behind traces on CCTV, on multiple wifi and cell networks, reporting in essence everywhere they have been and every time they stop, browse or enjoy a new experience. That data is in addition to the material they will consciously consume from video on demand, through their smart spectacles which overlay AR upon every surrounding from comparison shopping a supermarket shelf, and examining the freshness of the raw foods to providing all manner of data on the streets around as well as a constant flow of news about the markets as they walk around the office.

Gigabyte girls were the early adopters of rich social media like Instagram and Snapchat. That has given way swiftly to the terrabyte tribe who are becoming more digitally savvy but still probably don't realise how much data they leave behind on everything from web sites to subway machines about their everyday life. Naturally everybody today scoffs at the kilobyte generation who placed men on the moon... The notion that Apollo 11 was able to achieve lunar landing with less than the capacity of a conference freebie Fitbit clone today will be the equivalent of a digital fairy story for our child born today when they listen to bedtime fantasy tales in a few years time...

For the child today is not even a member of the petabyte people (they are already amongst us). Rather the child born today is at least, in data terms, likely to be a member of generation Exabyte – developing and deploying at least 1 000 000 000 000 000 000 Bytes of data during their lifetime... As things stand currently all human speech throughout history to date has probably amounted to about 5 exabytes. However our baby today is going to be de facto perma-tracked in multiple dimensions, sound, vision, and location amongst them, while in due course quantum computers will mine their data trails for all manner of insights intended to aid their health, wealth and happiness. Meanwhile some more totalitarian actors may equally use that data to stymie the liberty of our baby as they grow more mature.

Back to today's baby's relationship with money, it isn't just in how they will adopt natively to digital assets in every walk of life, nor that physical cash will be to them a novelty much like horse riding has become a hobby for many where it was the essential mode of transport only a few generations before. Indeed, it is hard to see how many established elements of our society can continue to serve today's baby. One key financial example will be the structural change to a staple of the 20th century for third agers, the old age pension. However, our baby born today joins a generation which will be lucky to see a pension much on the south side of a century.

Admittedly, even then they ought to get 30 years of leisure so it's surely not such a bad deal? – and of course the state's ability to provide a meaningful pension will have long since dwindled to, at best, a discredited pittance.

At home the level of domestic automation will finally be approaching the level envisaged in the sort of sci fi like the Jetsons which had occupied television screens only a handful of years before I was born. All this of course entails vast new data trails... It has been amusing to see the traditional cycle of media towards innovation in recent years. A few years ago the Internet of Things was being trumpeted as your best labour saving friend: your hob would be warming dinner up as you headed out of the subway while the intelligent kitchen tracked your commute home so that dinner was ready within minutes of returning... Presumably the 3D food printer was busy working on constructing a few colourful, nutritiously balanced side dishes too.

Within months a media driven to clickbait terror stories was busy noting how your IOT devices would soon be the source of hacker energy destined to undermine your very existence. Thus our baby today may find their kitchen of tomorrow is not a companion to while away the long winter's nights alone but actually could end up supporting their rival team, or just hoovering up domestic data to pass on to nefarious actors.

That said, doomsters have always been proven wrong – why should the digital age be any different? In the analogue era, Malthusians made much clamour about how the earth would run out of resources to feed humanity. Malthus' prognostications are now into a fourth century of being proven wrong while world population has gone from 800 million at the time of his dire warnings in 1798 to over 7.7 billion today. In modern times, much is made of the danger that digital life brings... yet in reality the benefits are simply colossal. Our child born today will be able to exploit data and live a life rich in benefits that were simply inconceivable even a century ago.

With this being a clearly digital generation, everything is different for the child born today. By contrast to my own birth a relatively few years earlier, the white heat of technology at that time was hardly dazzling by comparison – transistor radios and a few months wait before the Boeing 747 "jumbo" jet arrived, ushering in a new era of global travel. Where our baby will see a hugely decentralized digital lifestyle, my childhood was a heavily centralised experience – TV came from a trio of networks in Britain and the 'lucky ones' on the island of Ireland lived in Dublin where quirks of broadcasting distribution meant they received UK channel signals as well as the Irish ones... At best 8 or 9 channels broadcasting about 14 hours a day. Nowadays more content – 300 hours – than was available on those 8 or 9 channels viewable from Dublin are uploaded every minute to YouTube alone! Indeed, even in my teens my microcomputers were comfortably outpacing the processing power of Apollo 11 which landed men on the moon 50 years ago. The iPhone 5, outmoded today, had 1300 times more processing power than the first lunar mission... With this pace of development it can be easy to bicker when an app closes or a reboot is required but turning the clock back a couple of decades is like recollecting a relative dark age.

In our modern world – and let's face it that word, "modern" has been applicable for eons... But has any modernity felt as good as the digital modernity of today? I don't believe so. Our "modern" world is just an awesome time to be alive. I am surprised today's baby can sleep as the future looks even more exciting still!

Financial technology ("Fintech") like so much in our increasingly digital world, is in the midst of a profound revolution across every walk of life. And it is just getting started. There are too many new and exciting trends to list them all but having made it this far in the chapter, you get the gist: A short list might include cloud technology, software as a service, platforms as a service, blockchains, robotics, artificial intelligence, smart analytics and the looming pervasiveness of the Internet of Things. These all provide fertile ground for creative minds to come up with innovative solutions to real problems.

Moreover each area has its own financial-related dynamic... and that's before we look at competitive monies themselves in the form of cryptocurrency... Nor have we begun to consider that quantum computing potential which is not far away.

However we approach the wonders of this coming age, it will involve a subtly different relationship to money and finance. Often the new money relationship will be driven by new products and opportunities that were broadly impossible to imagine just a few decades ago. This is now an era where "TMA" will become the prevailing backbone of investment: "Trade Me Anything" products can be based upon pretty much anything that moves daily or less frequently, whether it grows, evolves, is elemental, or involves, any form of debt, equity and whatever optionality or payment structure you care to consider. That means your money, your assets can be based on anything, so long as the network can find a price...

The world of our baby born today has never looked so complex, nor has it ever offered so much opportunity. Whether you are a child or an adult, it is impossible to look at today's world and its vast opportunities without staring with a baby-like wonderment at the fabulous technology of it all...

2. The View From The Peak

"Yes, now you know. Now you know! That's what it was to be alive. To move about in a cloud of ignorance; to go up and down trampling on the feelings of those...of those about you. To spend and waste time as though you had a million years. To be always at the mercy of one self-centered passion, or another. Now you know — that's the happy existence you wanted to go back to.

Ignorance and blindness."

Simon Stimson from his grave in "Our Town" by Thornton Wilder

I want you to visualize your life in the palm of your hand. Actually better still, before you start thinking I have speared off into the world of self help books and go all uber-mindful: place your cellphone in your palm. Consider the role your smart device plays in your everyday existence and... hold on a moment:

Mission accomplished!

For a vast bulk of folks throughout the world, we have now achieved the simple step of placing pretty much our day and thus our life in one small device – a tiny box of tricks which compresses thousands of times more power than powered Apollo 11, the first spaceship to reach the moon. Actually one modern cell phone could power all the Apollo missions simultaneously and still have a lot of space left over for Instagram, Pinterest and Pokemon Go. The cell phone in its smartphone incarnation is a wondrous beast. Social media is there, the internet can be browsed from it, the wifi accesses your home / office / hotel / restaurant routers. In between WiFi hotspots, a 3/4/5g signal keeps you in touch with everything in your life. You can chat to folks on Telegram, WhatsApp and Hangouts.

Indeed you can deploy VOIP apps like Poivy for those who you need to reach but haven't realised that even the moderately geriatric (in digital terms) circuitry of Skype beats paying a phone company to talk to people. Perhaps even more radically still, on occasions the portable digital device now sitting in the palm of my hand emits a weird tone and vibrates maniacally. This, it transpires, is some old luddite who has rung a telephone number linked to my SIM card. How awesome is that? Multiple generations of technology in one device! Not only is this a full scale computer, database – including my personalised news stand and library, with audio recorder and playback – a digital Walkman if you can remember the 1980s... It is also a still camera – actually several still cameras depending on whether I want to record the world out there or concentrate on my personal position within the world, all without even rotating the smart device. Moreover it can deliver video recording and playback. Whole analogue tv networks worked for decades with less processing power than your cellphone. Now you can make a Vlog or podcast, edit it and post it online, all from a single 'phone.'

So here is this total life digital organiser document processor, communications tool (with a full multimedia editing suite) in the palm of my hand which records my receipts and spending alongside my boarding passes and train tickets. It is my personal bank branch, investment portfolio management tool, cryptocurrency wallet and membership card holder for many clubs (I can ping you my business card from there digitally too if your device is passing by). Then, as I said, the icing on the cake, there is even an old line telephone for those who still hark back as far as Basil Rathbone inviting his butler to bring in that crazy cup earpiece and speaker stand on a silver salver, checking not to trip over the cable or the tails of his housecoat. By comparison my digital life holder is wireless and can serve for days as my digital factotum without even needing an electrical charge.

The serious thing about the digital revolution is how the explosion of smart cell phones and tablets has radically reworked our entire way of life. In that sense, we're already reaching a fabulous switchover in existence and interface.

There are those who believe life is the laptop… which surpassed the once dominant desktop and almost unseen in contemporary everyday life "personal computer." The 'desktop' PC is nowadays broadly restricted to the fiefs of those concentrating upon high speed online gaming, digital print page design or video editing. They're a kind of totemic symbol of Twitch or pictorial design. By comparison, the transition to mobile devices has been achieved at remarkable speed. The iPhone emerged to instant public acclaim on June 29th 2007 and the modern smartphone era was upon us, rendering much of the Nokia / Erikkson and Motorola cell phone lineage instantly redundant. Within 5 years whether we were on Android or IoS, smartphones became semi-ubiquitous while a few hardy souls remained in a monogamous textual relationship with their Blackberry. The Canadian device wasn't as groovy as the smartphone but did a lot of decent word processing.

The development of the smartphone and its slightly bigger sibling the tablet, marked a massive shift for society. We became unchained from our desks and liberated to conduct all manner of transactions without having to be even in the office, or at home. This shifted power significantly for customer interactions. Moreover, it finally marked a peak in all manner of 'bricks and mortar' physical concepts which had to date weathered the storm of the internet. As things stand today, for many 'traditional' business elements we are in essence looking down from the peaks. We may be a little before or after the summit but certainly perspective shows a long rocky road down the other side towards a distance horizon beyond which it is difficult to discern what may lie next…

I would say the one guaranteed item on the horizon is opportunity. However, when facing "The Innovators' Dilemma," incumbent companies may prefer to try their luck standing on precipice of the peak, even if there is a lot of slippery gravel underfoot and a large chasm beneath. Let's examine how some peak industries are reacting...

Take banking for instance. Since pretty much time immemorial (well actually about 500 years in the 'modern' banking era), the clientele was used to visiting a fixed location and transacting their financial services from there. Indeed before that financial transactions had been centralised in a similar fashion for thousands of years if we delve back into the moneylenders in the Old Testament temples, or financial merchants of the agora and marketplaces further away in history to the likes of ancient Phoenicia. Finance has always relied on such clustering effects. This meant a point of heavy centralisation in particular districts, cities, or regions and beyond that our forefathers developed a network distributed across entirely physical branches with little intraday contact to the headquarters. This was a system which in more recent times allowed a local bank manager to have a certain prestigious standing in their home town. He (and it was almost always a "he" in those days) was an arbiter of fair minded fiscal services to the community. Nowadays, the concept of a bank branch is increasingly deliciously outmoded. I say deliciously because, let's face it, when was the last time you actually enjoyed queuing in a bank? Certainly nothing quite oozes user hostility like a bank branch. Given that they have been entrusted with your money, couldn't they be a bit more civilised? Can you honestly say your life was ever enhanced for more than a nanosecond (if even that) by reading the agitprop advertising posters on the walls? Pardon me for being picky but 'we'll give you a pittance for our money when you deposit it' never rang a chord with me, no matter how allegedly delightful the poster artwork. Moreover, if you have visited a bank of late did you even have a transactional human interaction? (Sub question – was the human interaction actually anything approaching humane?). True there are many banks with cheery greeters in the Walmart style who are perma-smiling and lovely to see but really as a means of intermediating access to an ATM, I'm not sure this always represents money well spent for the bank nor time well spent for the customer. Realistically, the only time you have been face to face with an actual bank employee in months has been to retrieve a card, or complete something which requires physical presence. In the latter case it is usually mortgage applications. The mortgage application remains a bizarrely sado-masochistic process designed to infuriate, obfuscate and generally just frustrate. As exercises in futile box ticking go, this one invariably earns a Kafka gold star. Moreover the peak of every property market reveals lots of stories about how mortgages were fraudulently obtained / granted – in every case I have to admire the fortitude of anybody who goes through such a process – certainly the old saying "honesty is the best policy" clearly is not an apt one for mortgage applications. Moreover, given the mortgage secures a property, I am pretty confident just rolling up a condo and taking it away under your arm is impractical, even if you're built like Samson. Nevertheless banks habitually behave when issuing mortgages as if this is precisely the borrower's intention.

The St Louis Federal Reserve Bank did some elegant research into the move from cell phones to smart phones. As the web-enabled device took off, so too the demand for online banking has accelerated and the bank branch has become rapidly disintermediated. How well banks have provided services or maintained customer relations with those whose branches have been closed is not the aim of this book. That said, I suspect the 'smart' money will settle on 'poorly.' For banks in retrenchment mode are rarely coherently managed with customer service aforethought. (How much customer service aforethought any modern bank can muster is a further topic still). Indeed quite why banks spend so much time trying to save money on the customer interface when their challenge is actually making the back end of the process work properly, is more perplexing still.

Thus with digital technology breaking the model of cashier culture from various angles, we are already past the point of peak bank branch. That drives all manner of interesting changes across society as well as finance itself. For one thing, the impact on the commercial real estate market is significant. The number of High Street banks is dwindling. Moreover, the lack of branches is changing the whole notion of footfall... That entirely alters the concept of the High Street. Traditionally, many vendors placed themselves close to banks. It was an ideal way to lure in shoppers of all hues when they went to the bank – particularly those who happened to have those most useful of purchase facilitators: money, or credit. The bank branch retrenchment process has a fundamental impact on the whole high street and thus clearly, also the dynamics and profitability of being a landlord. In the likes of Eastern Europe where many retail properties, especially in smaller towns and cities are still in the hands of private owners with modest (if not mono or micro) portfolios, it has been increasingly apparent that the rents landlords can expect for physical shop premises are not merely being damaged by the online shopping effect per se, there is now one less stable bellwether paying high rents... Moreover the general retreat from their previous high street prevalence of cell phone companies is another core rental customer fundamentally affecting the town centre and shopping mall respectively. In essence with mobile phones reaching saturation point, while they still have need of showrooms and shops, these are more customer retention points which can be concentrated amongst the modest oligopoly of brands in the relevant cell phone market as opposed to the many providers who all fought for market share in the earlier stages when 'virgin' customer acquisition was at the de facto gold rush stage of conversion to mobile telephony (and subsequently transitioning to smart phones). Now most everybody owns a smartphone there is less need for a multitude of showrooms. In a move of huge synergy which also works against High Street rentier landlords, by judiciously deploying smartphone apps, you can save some time. You no longer need to queue amidst the hordes being greeted (un)smilingly by front of house staff in a bank branch. Thus on a broader scale, provincial cities with once bustling high street stores are suffering the digital dash online of banks and retailers. Take the Staffordsire town of Burslem in Stoke on Trent which is bereft of free ATM machines as all the major banks have pulled out, leaving 44 out of 130 retail units empty during 2019. The path down from peak bank branch creates all manner of collateral damage…

This story is being replicated across the retail globe as these factors combine to create a major impact on the entire focus of the High Street and conventional 'bricks and mortar' retailing. After all the classic real estate mantra "location location location" depends on footfall. Footfall is clearly dictated by where people *need* to go… and indeed, *want to go*. As I mentioned previously, back in the times of analogue banking (well arguably there has been no change there!) before the networked digital web being close to the bank was in, and of itself, a vital retail location cherished and sought after by all means of shops. After all what better place was there on the High Street than being right beside the depository of clients' money? Being bereft of banks in a world of online banking even removes the stimulus for some to be on the High Street entirely… This leaves shoppers to virtually wander the web and choose AliExpress or Amazon and eBay as their chosen sources for much shopping.

Besides, my wife and I prefer doing almost all family grocery shopping online (apart from fruits / vegetables and other fresh food). Even a poor online shopping website for a supermarket – and we use a very elementary Maltese web 1.0 interface – is a vast improvement on actually traipsing through the store itself alongside a cornucopia of what one might on occasion have been able to term "the great unwashed" before the political correct era befell the liberal sense of humour. Whether it is feral pensioners or aimlessly bumbling children, stereotypical mall folks can be easily avoided by shopping digitally. Oh, and how many times has your car emerged from a shopping centre car park in better condition than it went in? Yip, thought so. What price is worth paying to avoid that hideous mall muzak alone? Even in Malta, we can battle the old website, secure the necessary comestibles in modest quantities and the delivery is free too. A little planning and supermarket visits can be expunged from your existence. Bliss? Well relief certainly. Time saved too. Thus when some standard staples of shopping digitize, the entire dynamic of defaulting to "just going to the High Street" are rapidly diminished in utility and thus in total footfall. Yes, there are still bakers and butchers, grocers and suchlike but the dynamics of a high street change when suddenly there is no bank at its core to be a major target of those who, by definition, have some money, or perhaps better still, access to credit... That completely alters the footfall dynamic. The notion of "let's place our upmarket sandwich deli beside the bank because the wealthier clients in town walk past there" simply disintegrates.. As does the rationale for positioning bigger ticket luxury item stores near banks... which means the accessory store no longer seeks to lurk around the corner in the cheaper streets nearby. ...All because the bank decided to go online and close the branch.

Technoology, it changes everything. As if you hadn't noticed...(when you probably bought this book online).

Back to your very own life. It's right there in the palm of your hand – the cellphone, with the power to launch a moonshot or two. That's how mega the cellphone has become. Unmanned deep space missions like the Cassini probe which lasted 19 years 335 days and reached Saturn required less computer power than many current Android games Thus the computing power right now in the palm of your hand is clearly a big big factor in finance because your handheld device can power your cash management, act as a payment device and indeed as I noted previously, deliver a multitude of other services. When I started in finance – not that long ago I hasten to add – the tool of that era's 'rocket scientists' was the Hewlett Packard HP-12C calculator first introduced in 1981. It is still available for purchase and takes a handy minute to do some calculations a simple spreadsheet can do semi-instantaneously upon hitting the return key. The H-12C has less power than a smart toaster nowadays and is the same size, indeed rather bulkier than your smartphone. Then again when they landed Apollo missions on the moon, the NASA engineering geeks often calculated everything on their slide rules... Whereas the HP-12C came with a massive instruction manual of functions, your smartphone is so intuitive that after a few moments of interaction, it enables any essentially digitally literate soul to hold their life in the palm of their hand, connecting to the world digitally via the interweb. This can run through cellular or wifi connectivity... Indeed as I type we're on the cusp of proper 5G gaining widespread network adoption: That means crunching, words, video and sounds at simply stunning speed. Thus where original benchmarks may have been how long it took to perform a particular mathematical function or engineering task, nowadays the popular benchmark for network speed is how rapidly it can download a cat video.

A key peripheral point to the hardware and its enabling networks delivering software process on the cellphone, is also the handy question of trust. Users trust their cellphones. We stuff them full of personal data, leaving mementoes like photos and much else on the device. Indeed we think nothing of letting it take our fingerprint to allow us access to a cavernous data vault... Folks who in person give grudging consent to being digitally fingerprinted by passport control at airports like New York JFK or Rafic Hariri International in Beirut willingly use it as the default means to access their smartphone built by people they don't know run by network operators they have never met. That's a big dollop of trust in a smartphone that is at heart, a dumb storage terminal.

If mobile telephone adaptation is changing the world of banking by driving bank branches to close, your smart cellphone is increasingly your investment centre too. Broker data (some shared privately alas I cannot divulge sources) all points to the same answer when it comes to how people want to trade or invest. While making no endorsement of brokers at the more speculative and leveraged end of the market per se, the device access picture is the same: a long downward sloping line from top left towards bottom right representing an operating system called Windows. For the many on Android, Linux or Apple IOS, a history lesson: Windows is still run by a company called Microsoft based in Redmond, Washington, USA near Seattle. Once upon a time Microsoft was pretty much the most powerful company on earth. Even as a more mainstream / niche brand today, it still has a market capitalisation north of a trillion dollars. For retail traders even in the relative technological backwater of Europe, there was a moment of singularity in early 2017 when Microsoft Windows was surpassed in favour of the mobile app culture which has since comprehensively eclipsed the once dominant PC-based operating system – in terms of accessing retail investor platforms. Whereas the desktop has long since ceded its prime position to the laptop, so too the digital device has become the most important communications cum processing tool on the planet... That means a tectonic shift where Google's Android is the biggest OS on the planet, powering a zillion mobile phones, heaps of tablets and not a few smaller laptops too. It squeaked ahead for the first time in March 2017 with 37.93% share of all OS compared to 37.91% for the legacy Windows which had dominated OS across pretty much all device types since the 1980's. Google's Android went from a mere 2.4% in 2012 to the lead in 5 years, demonstrating how smart devices took over the world in less than a decade.

That's another nifty thing about revolutions and particularly this wonderful world of technological upheaval – the pace of change and improvement of devices drives a faster cycle with new iterations dwarfing the previous versions. Moore's law of computer power might yet hit a wall in the next decade but it has proven a rather reliable indicator of computing power. If you cannot recall how your computer has changed since the 1990's, then go back to the palm of your hand and recall what your phone could do for you in 1995, or even 2005, compared to today's gadgets that power your life for a day or more without even needing to be recharged as often as their human masters need a recuperative sleep.

This sort of upheaval has been building over the past 2 decades creating a reign of terror amongst the likes of banks and other legacy financial providers. True banks have the advantage of their exalted regulatory monopoly to maintain a greater regulatory stranglehold on matters. Nevertheless it is clear the world has moved toward mobile investment access. Once again, that changes everything. We are all mobile now – in multiple senses! When it comes to how technology can leapfrog generations, we only need to consider the way the digital revolution has played out. Those with copper wires looked outmoded when fibre optic cable emerged. Thus TransAtlantic cable laid by the Isambard Kingdom Brunel designed SS Great Eastern in 1866 was ultimately usurped – albeit a century and a half later! – by the likes of Project Kelvin (linking Ireland to the USA and continental Europe since 2010 with 40 Gigabits per second capacity) and the 2017 blue riband link from USA to Bilbao, Spain, Project Marea, transporting a scintillating 160 terabits of data per second. As extremetech.com mentioned at the time with studied understatement "That's rather a lot." Or to put it in slightly better context: this amounts to around 15 times the entire catalogue of printed material in the US Library of Congress. Every second. Even measured in pawsecs of cat video, most of the world's telegenic tabbies can be captured with alarming regularity. Incidentally, Marea was backed by Facebook and Microsoft so clearly there is a future to Microsoft even if its monopoly OS days are behind it. At launch (its modular design enables significant upgrade potential) Marea was roughly 16 millions times faster than the 'high speed' internet in most European homes. Thus Kelvin was roughly a multiplicity of the regional Ulster parliament's political Hansard every second whereas Marea is 71 million high definition videos streaming simultaneously. As always with internet statistics, how many of these HD streams at any one time are cat videos is open to debate.

These rather mind-boggling quantities of data transfer enabled by the laying of cables expose the physical frailty of physically connecting vast distances. In that respect, many land masses left behind by the copper to fibre optic revolution opted to leapfrog straight to mobile. In some ways that meant communications transmission had gone full circle: transAtlantic telephone calls were originally carried by radio waves in 1927. This avoided vast geographical areas which were hard to physically lay cable across (whether due to extreme habitat conditions or neighbourhood instability). This has given rise to a whole new quantum of data delivery over mobile and satellite networks with data centres being built below the mobile communications towers which capture the mobile signals. Thus payments providers such as M-Pesa have progressed fintech in Africa and delivered incredible leaps forward in commercial activity all by deploying little more than a robust smart app on a cellphone which itself uses cellphone driven data centres, all with a paucity of any form of fixed cable... In many areas of the continent, Africa essentially leapfrogged from all but zero telephony to being on a world standard that enabled not merely voice traffic but data traffic which is a building block to expanding commerce.

Given that the broad media is usually a festival of ongoing negativity (apparently it increases the audience – not that this is evident from waves of media redundancies in recent years), it may at first appear almost counterintuitive to believe the following... However, whatever may occur in the short term economically, the simple reality is that technology and its ongoing process improvement and miniaturisation are elements of a hugely bright future for humanity and planet earth. It is indeed highly feasible we have a recession to get through before we re-emerge into the blinking sunlight of a new growth cycle whereupon the whole next leg evolves with gusto. Then again in the coming phase we are looking at an incredible possibility as nanotech and biotech shapes a whole new world. Moreover, just as our child born today knows, the future of the world is going to be shaped by the way we deal with and interact with money – albeit that relationship is going to be a lot more virtual than it has ever been before....

Therefore we are looking down from the peak of bank branches – the physical peak of banking per se – along with peak mobile phone store and the peak of all manner of physical points of commerce.

Looking out over the landscape of technology in general and fintech specifically, it is incredibly difficult not to be superbly optimistic about the opportunities ahead for everyone in society, everywhere on earth. Of course there is much to be concerned about but this book is written against a backdrop of 5 people emerging from poverty around the world every second. An overseas flight was an event worthy of bringing the family to wave folks off at the airport only a few decades ago... Nowadays discount airlines vie with coach companies on price and enable travels far beyond what was attainable back in the old analogue days of greater regulation & lesser technology during the 1960s / 1970s. Such commoditization has vastly aided travel. Meanwhile on a higher level still, biotechnology and nanotechnology as well as the wonders of the interweb enable all manner of communication through medical advances which were the stuff of science fiction when I was born. I hasten to point out that birth was not so long ago either!

In essence we're at peak bank, peak bank branch, peak shop and much else besides but the great thing about the Schumpeterian process of creative destruction is, provided government allows the process to run its course, the next wave is always faster, cheaper and better for consumers and investors alike.

The economy may still vary as it must through multiple cyclical encounters and there are always things to complain about – not just the state of banks – but the world is moving forward and that's cause for optimism. In finance, we have greater power at our fingertips to borrow, lend and invest than we have ever had before. The post banking world is coming close, enabling us to avoid the need to deal with the atrophied legacy financial system.

3. The Magic Post It Note

"We should think about the blockchain as another class of thing like the internet. A comprehensive information technology with tiered technical levels and multiple classes of applications for any form of asset registry, inventory and exchange, including every area of finance, economics and money; hard assets (physical property) and intangible assets (votes, ideas, reputation, intention, health, data, information etc.)."

Melanie Swan, founder Institute for Blockchain Studies

One of the wondrous things about massive laboratories in multinational companies is their ability to let the pointy-headed classes roam free with their inventive genius. One particularly talented researcher in the field, a chemist called Dr John Silver was so singularly successful, he even changed the world through his failure! In 1968, his task was to invent a super strong glue.

Of course this task ought not to be confused with what is termed Superglue. That had its origins in a completely different failed experiment during 1942 in the Rochester New York Eastman Kodak labs. At the time they were trying to design plastic gun sights for the war effort. Using cyanoacrylates proved frustrating as they stuck to everything immediately and permanently... In 1951 having moved to the Eastman Kodak chemical lab in Kingsport, Tennessee, the same chemist previously based in Rochester, Harry Coover, noted the persistently frustrating property when discarding these cyanoacrylates as a means to develop heat resistant polymers for aircraft canopies. However it struck him there was a use to this strong bonding agent. By 1958 the patented Eastman 910 was on the market... Superglue became a huge seller. It was even deployed to bond emergency wounds in the battlefield during the Vietnam war as those with large bleeding injuries were usually dying before they could reach any form of field hospital.

With Superglue proving popular, many firms were looking for their own version of strong instant adhesive during the 1960's. In one failed experiment Dr Silver ended up with a very weak consistency. This 'adhesive' – and I use the term loosely in every respect – made a connection but was easy to pull apart and reaffix, even to a different object. Whereas it took Harry Coover two interactions with cyanoacrylates to discern their enormous potential, upon first, er, contact, Silver reckoned he had the solution to something. The only sticking point was Dr Silver just wasn't sure precisely what problem he had solved. So John Silver promoted his rather limp adhesive internally at 3M for no less than five years! Fret not we haven't abandoned the narrative thrust of fintech. Moreover, we'll return to Dr Silver in a paragraph...

Having been a fintech advocate since, as I have noted, way before we even had the word fintech, it has often been noticeable that folks will ask pertinent questions while being a touch, er, cloudy on the underpinnings of what is being discussed. Most of the time that is no bad thing. We don't have to understand the moments of vibration for balancing car engines to effect a safe drive to visit family and friends. However, when talking about blockchain, some knowledge of its basic theory at least, is hugely beneficial. Thus it's best to have a basic understanding of how the distributed ledger works in order to follow what it can do for you, how it can help your business and perhaps most significantly of all, why it makes all previous disintermediary tools in history look like mere droplets on the windshield. In essence DLT represents a tsunami wave of potential disruption. It may also be pertinent to understand the basics before your bank or exchange group spends a 7 or 8 figure sum on investing in a DLT/Blockchain consortium. However for many institutions that ship already appears to have sailed a few years back.

Back to Dr Silver, his tenacity with products using his somewhat lacklustre and hence not very SuperGlue at all, adhesive, proved a masterstroke. At this juncture in the narrative, we ought to pause for a moment and veritably praise the Lord! Art Fry, a 3M colleague of Dr Silver's was finding it frustrating singing in the church choir. At invariably inconvenient harmonic moments, his bookmarks kept falling out of his hymn book. Recalling Dr Silver's weak adhesive, Fry conducted his own choral experiment. The result was easier bookmarking for the movable feast of singing opportunity which is the weekly church service. Armed with a selection of different hymns and bookmarks which stayed in place through the service but could be easily re-positioned for the following Sunday, Art Fry was a happy chorister.

Thus the sticky note gained traction towards becoming a bestseller. Coincidentally, the yellow benchmark colour of the product which became "Post-it" notes in 1980 was as a result of a stockpile of canary yellow scrap paper. A discounted launch nationwide using recycled paper fuelled a globally recognised brand colour. Post It notes became a stationery phenomenon ubiquitously affixed to fridges worldwide – enabling recipe notes, school reminders, notes between partners on different shifts… a whole new means of easy messaging and reminders! Post Its delivered an easy means to bookmark all manner of documents with comments, or points at which signatures were required. In the late analogue era of 'peak paper,' Post-Its spawned derivatives in a broad range of formats, right through to funky shapes and licensed variations. Few children could survive a consumerist childhood in the world's wealthier environs during the 1990s without a portfolio of suitably branded and/or crazily shaped sticky notes.

At this point it is worth noting that Blockchain doesn't come shaped like a cat, a heart or any other Post It note format, nor (despite some Dilbert cartoon suggestions) does it come in a particular colour). However a Blockchain – a Distributed Ledger – is in essence a form of magic sticky note. (True, some DLTs have a relationship to crypto kitties but that is an entirely different story).

In essence a database is another form of ledger – a digital ledger in effect. Databases are essentially digitised centralised ledgers. When we have a ledger and make an amendment on it, say by adding a post-it, then the sticky note is only visible to whoever added the note and reads that particular ledger. Now that can be a handy means of communication for, say, the auditor to leave a note querying something for the book keeper within the office. However if we are talking about a large corporation, or any relationship where it is tricky to pass a physical ledger, then clearly this becomes troublesome. Of course with computerisation there was the option to make a note on the file then save the file and send it to the other person (originally on a disk, later by email) at which point the person could open the ledger file, read the virtual post-it note and then go back through the same rigmarole of saving the file... It wasn't quite Sisyphean but it resulted in multiple copies of ostensibly the same documents, all with frustratingly minor iterative discrepancies.- and no core narrative record.

This process then moved forward with the development of cloud computing. Here the document could be stored in a cloud file (e.g. simply through Google Drive) and then the note left on the file was effectively shared with all parties who have access rights to the file.

So far so good... but clearly the worry still arises of how a digital document can be different from one place to another. Most notably the concern a file can be modified without another party noticing... True modern software has means to track changes but it is a fiddly and time consuming business. Besides, it offers no protection to those who wish to change a file for their own ends.

Now consider this curious hybrid beast, part database and part something more exotic still which some call the blockchain. In one sense Blockchain exists in its own form of dissipated digital universe. In other words it is distributed across different points of presence – or nodes. So in that sense it is like a "super-cloud" kind of app – and hence the less prosaic name for blockchain: Distributed Ledger Technology (I will abbreviate that to DLT for simplicity). At the same time, the DLT / Blockchain offers something additionally on top of all this which truly delivers a third dimension. This byproduct is a facet of trust inducement which is rather radical and, like so many great technology innovations, a tad uber-nifty at the same stroke.

This is where a blockchain becomes what I term a "Super-Post-it" note. Imagine if you will that when you spot something in the paper ledger in the accounts in your office in Los Angeles you want to make an amendment or add a note which shows:

1. A query or amendment;
2. Notifies everybody who has access to that document;
3. Makes an immutable change (i.e. the record of your query or change stays forever on the record);
4. And is immediately shared with everybody, regardless of where they are in the world, who is authorised to read or add data to this ledger.

Welcome to the world of the super Post-It note. Or DLT as it is more popularly known. When you add the data to your super-Post-it from your office in say, London, Seoul or Sydney…within the speed of data transfer (some fraction of a second) every node on the blockchain pulses with news of your amendment. The interweb hums with data and hey presto – every single node on the network updates with the same data you just entered. Moreover, remember, that amendment is now time stamped and saved on the network at every single node. Whoever can access the ledger can read what you said and moreover – when you said it… and that record is immutable, thus reducing the risk of fraud or tampering with a single ledger.

This is the point where a blockchain gains the sort of super power skill which if it could breathe Marvel would devote a comic to it. First of all there is the trust element. If you know every change that happens in the ledger is recorded and time stamped, then it generates trust. Moreover, trying to hack or change the ledger is much more difficult than merely changing an entry in one computer file. If you aren't on the network everywhere (a tricky distribution for a human) you would have to hack simultaneously (and by simultaneous I mean to an often infinitesimal fraction of a second) the entire network – every single node – AND manage to amend all the different documents precisely the same – to the last punctuation mark. To put it very mildly indeed, that's awfully tricky. Therefore, trust is an elegantly created byproduct because the network is no longer under the suzerainty of a single person or entity. The distributed nature of the ledger means the data is decentralised. Of course decentralisation scares big entities like, say, government, which enjoys nothing more than a judicious slice of control. However, many folk like the idea of a decentralised system where there is considerable security to stop one rogue person having control or modifying records to their fraudulent benefit. Governments are starting to see the benefit too as it makes it much trickier for folks to steal or amend government data in any one single place / time. That can be useful for housing records and indeed with the likes of medical records, suitable permissioning could mean the optician only has to see the pertinent parts of your record whereas your gynaecologist doesn't generally need to know the information your opthamologist requires.

Thus it is incredibly difficult to commit the equivalent of a bank robbery on a distributed ledger as there is no single point where the money can be grabbed. Rather the major point of weakness is where folks carelessly leave money in a single digital node – AKA their wallet – and get essentially crypto–pickpocketed. As in all great heist movie plots, robbing banks only works well when the cash is left in a single place. When any asset is distributed to the point where you have to break into several branches and or vaults simultaneously (again: to within the same fraction of a second), it all becomes rather complex....

Hence a blockchain is in one sense 'just' another database – where the context of 'just' is admittedly akin to glossing over his great sonnets by saying "William Shakespeare 'just' wrote words."

Distributed Ledger is a phenomenally smart piece of technology because it can be accessed universally (subject to permissioning). Simultaneously it decentralizes the storage of data to multiple different nodes while creating a time stamped, immutable record of amendments and modifications such that the blockchain delivers an elegant solution to all forms of provenance and record keeping.

Call it a super Post-it, if you will. Or you can construct medieval metaphors around the likes of tally sticks – pieces of wood used as records of payments to the exchequer. In England the tally sticks were made of hazel wood and described in "The dialogue of the Exchequer" by the Bishop of Ely, Richard fitz Nigel (1130-98). This book was a treatise on royal finances compiled for Henry II (r. 1154–89) and the author noted: "Let me briefly explain how tallies are made … The length of a lawful tally is from the tip of the index finger to the tip of the outstretched thumb." With the tally stick split, the government representative kept one side and the taxpayer the other – reuniting the sticks at the point of tax collection. In one sense, this too is a decent proxy for the basic discussion of the distributed ledger albeit on a very simple single transaction bilateral level.

We'll delve deeper into the world of DLT as the book progresses but for now a magic sticky note is a decent proxy to understand the technology itself…

4. 1000 BP A Bankers Lament

"[Bankers!] Cheer up the worst is yet to come."

[After] Philander Johnson

Remarkably, the all too often broadly incompetent and recklessly managed cabal of money stewards also known as banks have managed to become even more loathed by 2019 than they were in 1999. One feels almost inclined to applaud their effort. However, cheer up the good news is we're past one key tipping point. More on that later. Meanwhile technological progress, thanks to the ongoing fulfillment of Moore's law of processing power is helping accelerate the 'shock of the new' process in financial services. True, Moore's law – which postulated that a doubling of computer power every 18 months was plausible from the 1960's – is expected to run out of steam in around 2025. However that ought to be enough time to do a fair bit more damage to analogue incumbents in a good few other industry sectors. Banks have at least some protection in their balance sheets – albeit in some regions those don't look too healthy either.

Driving the key change factor in this new environment is not just the ongoing power of technological progress but also the brave new world of commoditised payments. In a world where the microprocessor has become king, everything has been reduced to a relevant micro-size. Thus micropayments which were pretty much theoretical when I outlined them in "Capital Market Revolution!" are now a reality staring every large ticket charging incumbent in the face across a range of commercial relationships. Way back then I noted a study by Frost and Sullivan in their March 1998 Telecoms Newsletter...

Person to Person In Branch transactions 1.95
ATM transactions 0.80
Telephone Banking Transactions 0.60
Internet Banking Transactions 0.20
E-cash transactions 0.01

Compare that to a colleague who recently had a veritable rant about how Transferwise, the high quality UK based payment service provider was charging 0.60 pence or slightly more on cross border transactions, leaving my millennial friend in meltdown. That's how far we have travelled in 20 years. Nowadays customers expect micropayment (or free!) transactions and of course they reckon money moves in almost real time. Two decades ago transactions between most UK banks were taking 3 days to conclude (albeit I seem to recall having a Barclays account at the time where more or less all transactions seemed to end up in the wrong place having taken considerably longer). However, now payments have hit an interesting zone – where the legacy payment systems have proven not only expensive (15-30+ dollar SWIFT transaction fees and your money could go 'dark' for days while banks blamed each other for whatever had disappeared in the messy old fashioned ways money did or didn't get transferred). Given that the good folks of UPS can nowadays geolocate a physical copy of this book from the printers to its destination in almost real time...it...provides a little colour on the ancient nature of SWIFT's networks. Thus speed and time are the nexus which create a whole new realm of money & banking adding flexibility to an archaic system where some apparent civilizations still deem cheques a nifty concept...

Equally, it is only fair to note that in the case of transfers, hidden costs remain a huge bugbear. In a classic example of the advertising art, Transferwise made a magnificent comparison of charges in 2017.

"What they tell you it costs to send 1,000 Pounds to Europe"[1]
The bare fees were as follows (all prices in Pounds):
Transferwise: 4.98
Western Union 2.90
Natwest 10.00
HSBC 2.67
Lloyds Bank 0.00
Paypal 0.00

In the advertisement, this was lined in yellow Lego bricks on a straight running track for barefoot sprinters.

Next they lined up a series of red bricks with "What it really costs with their exchange rates." This came out as:

Transferwise 4.98
Western Union 18.88
Natwest 33.88
HSBC 40.35
Lloyds Bank 41.50
Paypal 74.41

Needless to say in the advertisement, the Transferwise runner skips forward at the start with a first stride that takes him comfortably across the yellow bricks. The other runners endure periods of agony as they endeavour to tread across the prickly Lego bricks preventing them from running freely along the track...

It's a good example of hidden costs – and a salutary reminder that where the financial industry labels something as 'free' it usually means 'laden with hidden cost.' A good example being the stock trading business where some apps now claim you can have commission free trading in shares – a tricky thing to resolve as there

1. https://www.youtube.com/watch?v=iybKYj3OoXQ

are costs to transacting any stock so there must be some element of hidden fee being levied... applying the Amazon founder's line "Your margin is my opportunity" must be sufficient to deliver a high level of 'Bezosian' salivation greater than Pavlov's pooch could ever produce.

In essence, the headline figure of 4.98 may not have been spectacular for Transferwise in 2017 but at the same time, it was transparently cheaper than other providers still deploying legacy approaches to moving money.

Yet of course even 4.98 on a 1000 pound move is a huge fee compared to say derivatives markets where a million dollar contract can be obtained for a couple of dollars or less on almost every market. If you're a professional it's more like nickels and dimes at big futures exchanges such as ICE. However the trend from an equivalent of the analogue era where the fees alone were 20+ Pounds and the hidden forex costs the same or worse does represent a considerable reduction. Moreover with transparent forex platforms now common, the ability to reduce forex 'drag' further must now be the major issue for financial intermediaries who intend to survive the next wave of fintech.

Micropayments as the baseline in every financial process remains bad news for pretty much every current intermediary still within the financial value chain who remain wired to higher margin, higher overall levels of charging for a markedly worse (slower, less efficient), service. At the same time, incumbents – even those with a large regulatory cushion delivering a de facto monopoly – will survive for a while but not in the long term unless they can manage to radically rework their operational foundations. Here we see a subtle change in the revolution per se. While I will continue to argue that exchanges are missing more opportunities than they can manage to exploit, their overall development in the eye of the revolution during the past decade has been remarkable. Exchanges are no longer a core part of the problem as they were when Capital Market Revolution! was written. Rather the leading exchanges have helped point the way to the solution. To that end, the business of other intermediaries often looks rather worrying – or distinctly expensive if you are a consumer thereof. In the realm of pure exchange trading, electronic brokers and intermediaries have made remarkable progress during the past two decades, as I believed they would. The "Schwabification" of the world led by eTrade, Charles Schwab, IBKR et al has progressed digital brokerage to a point where it is essentially simple, seamless and cheap for anybody, retail investor or professional trader, to access the world's major markets from anywhere in the world. If only banks had evolved as exchanges and market platforms have, in terms of cost and customer accessibility! True, there are services 'designed' as internet banking but most are only carbuncles on the face of an aged structure from the era when technological forefront implied funding the stagecoach industry to transport cash. With electric vehicles now finally assuming control of the roads from internal combustion-engined cars, banking still needs to find a way to make the quantum leap from the equine epoch of transport to the drone age.

In several outwardly advanced nations, the US and Malta amongst them, banks still provide some truly quaint period pieces masquerading as services. Take the check/cheque for instance. It has origins dating back to the Mauryan period (321-185 BC). During that era an instrument called the adesha was an order requesting a banker to pay money to a third party. The Romans had their own form of cheque, the praescriptiones in the first century BC. Bear in mind at this time while cheques may have been circulating, what we would nowadays term paper, was still 200 years from being invented in China. (Somewhere in this narrative we will get to Alipay et al). Persians began issuing letters of credit around the 3rd century AD. These were called čak, meaning "document" or "contract." They later evolved into the sakk. This became a popular form of early cheque across Arab lands enabling a cross border cheque service which the modern world largely managed to lose as banks became national or local (even when multinational entities) and absorbed within national cheque clearing systems. The Venetians used bills of exchange in the 13th century while the Dutch brought the cheque concept forward in the early 1500s with 'cashiers.' Essentially those holding deposits of cash, began issuing additional services including the payment of money to any person bearing a written order from a depositor to do so, keeping the note as proof of payment. The Bank of England pioneered the use of cheques on a pre-printed form, using "cheque paper." To prevent fraud customers had to attend in person to collect a numbered form from the cashier.

Quite why in a digital world, it is still commonplace for some businesses to send money in the form of cheques is open to question. Some say because they are free at the point of issue in some countries….albeit once you actually post them in that quaint old service the mail… they are usually immediately more expensive than modern money transfers. Realistically the reason cheques remain popular is because their clearing time delays the money being eased out of the payer's bank account in favour of the payee. Thus we see one of the modern banes of efficient business in action – the curse of the delaying corporation (and generally speaking the larger the corporation the longer you wait for payment – a shameful state of affairs for all creditors, especially those with less than multinational balance sheets). Nowadays I perceive cheques more as an instrument by which corporations try to keep money from creditors for longer… Nevertheless, the fact that the banking system continues to even bother with the concept of paper money in the form of cheques is a profound oddity in 2019 AD! If you don't think cheques are bizarrely archaic, consider asking your physician for a dose of leeches next time you seek an ailment cure – that particularly popular remedy for medieval illnesses, i.e. maladies occurring a handy millennium after the earliest versions of the čak.

While ancient precepts and approaches like cheques are one part of the banking problem, in truth the major problem for banks is a mix of cost and their business model which are under simultaneous threat.

Returning to the question of cost, the problem for banks is the classic "Innovator's Dilemma" problem outlined by Clayton Christiansen in his fascinating book. Each chapter essentially told the same story. One for instance examined how Kodak recognised the impending arrival of digital photography but struggled with its addiction to the cash-flow from cellulose triacetate-based "Safety" films. Hence it fudged and ultimately all but disappeared from public view after spending much of its recent history with restructuring advisors in and out of bankruptcy, saddled with debt.

This Innovator's Dilemma is a core problem facing banks today. Banks have many potentially useful lines of business but need to find a way to offer a service while taking the hit from providing this better service in a new micropayment way where previously they have enjoyed massive quasi-monopoly rents as a byproduct of the exalted regulatory privilege. The difficulty remains that for all their attempts to speak a modern tale, often deploying naive or shameless hipsters as their de facto digital tiding bearers, walking the walk of modernity appears beyond the long-term profit sustainable reach of many legacy banks. Indeed banks mis-price one key risk to their model. There is a fixation in banking circles that banks are deemed safe by the public, ergo they cannot lose that trust of their clients. Therefore providing they behave in a generally bank-like fashion suggests a heady cocktail of social superiority, implying safety. Wrap it behind enough classical Georgian columns, the theory goes and the sucker public will stay loyal to the banking system. This analysis, while widespread in the banking industry misunderstands several things. For one banks aren't actually deemed especially safe by their customers. Rather the clients perceive a certain safety in deposit insurance schemes which governments place around deposit taking institutions in order to encourage saving (and thus the benefits of fractional reserve banking). In other words another example of bankers' exorbitant regulatory privilege. This misunderstanding on the part of banks that their clients 'trust' them is of course spectacularly underlined in many countries. It has been described deliciously by Metro Bank founder Vernon W Hill II, who noted that British banks' trust of their customers extended to the point where they chained the pens to the desk in the branch. Likewise, a branch structure probably imbued loyalty back in the day when the bank manager was at the epicentre of local life. However nowadays branches are in the main robotic structures with little leeway – all sense of the personal has been squeezed out of any interaction. Equally being haughty about money won't cut it for banks in an era where even stockbrokers have frequently adopted a stance which is as digital as banks remain difficult to like, particularly in an era where banks have become paranoid about their clients' transactions.

Beyond clients being broadly mistrusted, there are simple insanities which suggest banks have entirely lost the plot of their social and business purpose. While there are good arguments for replacing cheques, it became clear to me that the banking system had reached a new height of absurdity a few years back. At that time I needed to pay a particular utility and they demanded the payment was made in a bank branch to create immediate third party proof of payment. True enough this was Poland where the bureaucracy remains a semi perma-stifling Kafka-esque catastrophe on many levels. Where there are some sound utilities, equally the nation is saddled with some simply hideously inept entities. Thus in some bloated bureaucracies utterly sub third world standards prevail. ENERGA Obrot could arguably be renamed "Kafka's electric co" and it would still not do justice to my unpleasant experiences batling the customer oblivious, shambolic billing and payments regimen masquerading as a corporation. The precise reason we had to pay this bill escapes me...dealing with entities such as Energa often results in a form of Post Traumatic Stress Disorder to blank out the pain of their giddyingly asinine process. Anyway, the bizarre scenario that played out at the bank will remain forever etched on my memory. Armed with the bank details, the woman cashier had no problem accepting cash to pay the bill as a deposit but she made it clear I would have to pay for the privilege. Not, I hasten to add a payment processing fee or something. No, rather I was committing the mortal sin of depositing cash into a bank.

Think about that for a second.

I – was – depositing – cash – into – a – bank – and – I – needed – to – pay – for – the – privilege.

Yip, no frills discounters eat your heart out. Here was the ultimate in financial absurdity – a bank that didn't like taking, er, money. Even ostensibly customer oblivious discount airlines haven't quite managed to go that far. (but I suspect they have pangs of jealousy at this banking masterstroke).

Once a bank had decided it needed to levy a charge for money being given to it, I was given to a fanciful fit of thought on what might be next? Would, for example, water services begin invoicing clouds for the cost of depositing H2O in reservoirs? Seriously, at the time when a company no longer accepts the very folding stuff which its entire raison d'etre revolves around, it was readily apparent that not only were we past the peak of banking but indeed rapidly accelerating down the slippery slope of obsolescence.

It's not just the dismal products, the mediocrity of customer service or the mismanagement of compliance function which is killing banking. Of course it is the cost. Thus banking is at the epicentre of a perfect storm which is driving its retreat notwithstanding a highly engaged ability of management to seemingly engineer their own obsolescence through repeatedly ham-fisted management decisions – and I don't even mean the dodgy lending which emerges as every economic upturn wanes and turns into the recessionary side of the cycle.

While nowadays apparently banks are pro actively isolating themselves from the concept of actually accepting legal tender as part of their business process, it appears banks seek to charge at every vestige of any process. At this rate any branches still open by 2025 will probably charge customers for the receptionists' smiling. Come to think of it, some may say with justification the era of a free smile at a bank branch has long since evaporated anyway... Worse still than having to pay for everything, the quality of their intermediation leaves a great deal to be desired. UK High Street banking has historically proven a form of Russian roulette of service ineptitude. Customers, even in the UK's slightly odd arena of many 'free' banking basic services, are used to a life of suffering as opposed to service with many of the domestic providers. Everywhere, banks expect to charge fees and take haircuts with a verve that leaves clients close to bald on every front. In that respect traditionally many customers blamed the remarkable concentration of "Big Three" "Big Four" or "Big Five" banking, a state of oligopoly which emerged in many nations such as Japan (3), Australian/New Zealand and the UK (4) and Canada (5).

Somewhat counterintuitively, banks apparently see no shame in profiting from printing money in certain areas, then charging you for the privilege of accepting the same currency in your bank account. There is some logic in this but it is a bit twisted if it is allowed to roam free as a long-term means of encouraging customer loyalty. In the days of de facto oligopolistic concentration that might have been manageable with some hypocritical chutzpah but in the modern era, the competitive pressures of parabanking alternatives such as payment services providers is simply too great to allow the banks to maintain their erratic ways unchallenged.

So, for one thing bank charges are, frankly, outrageous in a modern micropayments world. One only has to move money across borders to be subject to rather ridiculous charges.

In the world of foreign exchange, you can trade a million dollars as a retail investor for under 20 dollars, or indeed an exchange can transact a million dollar Eurodollar deposit for barely a dollar 50, yet move 5000 US dollars from one bank to another overseas and the danger lurks that a charge could still amount to easily the equivalent of at least 20 US dollars and of course that is before the banks commit an egregious 'hair cut' by changing money from one currency to another at a rate which is not far away from the licensed bandits operating all too many foreign exchange bureau in many European cities and airports.

True some improvements have taken place in recent years. In the Eurozone, the ECB has been rather inventive in creating a cost effective real-time payment service, TIPS, the TARGET instant payment settlement (TIPS) service which was rolled out late in 2018. TIPS enables banks and payment service providers to offer fund transfers in real time and around the clock, 365 days a year. The European Central Bank, as well as offering some free incentives at launch, was providing TIPS at 0.002 Euros, i.e. 2 tenths of a Euro cent. Of course this is another quasi-disaster for banks, as even if they charge a 10 times markup, they are making little or nothing from the process and as such TIPS is – perhaps counterintuitively, another nail in the coffin for banks themselves! However for newcomers to the payments field – of which there are many – the delivery of TIPS is another delightful opportunity to take micropayment advantage and profit while providing cheap customer services.

In essence banking is stuck in a rut where the systems are based on archaic pricing structures (often involving archaic precepts and technology) and without any remote proximity to the frontiers of digital finance. That the management of banks is personified by a variety of highly paid executives who believe they have a near God-given right to be bailed out by government when their management proves incapable, is hardly surprising. However bankers understand one key issue: they can extend their careers pretty much to their expiry date by playing on the relationship with government and exploiting the regulatory advantages given to banks to in essence speculate with other people's money.

Foreign exchange is another good example of the overcharging of banks as a norm. With a house in Poland, I have long since dispensed with the services offered within a bank for transferring currency. Rather it pays me to move, say US dollars from my bank to a separate third party payment provider and then back again to the another currency (e.g. Sterling, Euros or Polish Zloty) accounts with the original bank. The fact that I have had bank accounts with institutions in Poland which were less competitive for foreign exchange than the independent 'Kantor" kiosks exchanging notes in the centre of most Polish cities tells you everything you need to know about why banking has failed.

With a striking ability to extort frankly monopolistic rents in all manner of charges, it is also disturbing to take a long look at just how woefully uncompetitive banks are from yet another angle with their core lifeblood: money. As we all know, except in certain exceptional times, most currencies will yield a rate of interest when saved and indeed we can expect to be charged a rate of interest when we borrow. In money markets, the rates of interest applied to wholesale borrowers through short term liabilities such as commercial paper, government bills and longer term corporate and government bonds, demonstrate – ceteris paribus remarkably low and indeed competitive margins for lending. Just as electronic markets have bid/offer spreads that are frequently wafer thin on exchanges, so too the competitive lending environment in bills, bonds and other obligations mean that relatively speaking, yields are low and the spreads narrow for borrowers and lenders.

Once that borrowing/lending equation starts to trickle down within a bank however, the picture is somewhat different. Indeed this has become a longstanding farce debasing the wealth of the average worker at the expense of those who could best engage with various asset bubbles during the 21st century to date. This is all thanks to the ridiculous 'funny money' activities promulgated by central bankers who have perfected the 'heads the banks win, tails the customers lose' farce of quantitative easing – pumping money into the system to the point where banks have been vastly subsidised (on top of the egregious bailouts) for nigh on 20 years at the time of writing. Sadly these super low interest rates haven't even done much for the economy in many parts of Europe as, apart from being rendered quasi-moribund by anti-enterprise governments, the banking system has been broadly trying to merely survive, patching chronically holed balance sheets as a result of banker hubris in the period up to 2008.

Then we get to the simplest breakdown of the banking business model. At the epicentre of banking is a conceit which is no longer remotely viable. It works like this:

Take your cash and deposit it in the bank. If you have been in dollars, euros, Yen, Pounds Sterling, or Swiss Francs (which amount to over 90% of central bank reserves) or indeed Canadian and Australian or New Zealand dollars, amongst others then you have broadly thus far in the 21st century, at the time of writing, been unable to get more than a paucity of percent (usually one percent or less) per annum on your savings.

So cash deposited at the bank earns basically nothing in this day and age.

Now looking at the opposite side of the equation, try to borrow money from your bank / owe money on your credit card or overdraft. Suddenly banks easily find it quite normal to charge something in the double figures. Indeed US credit cards (source Wallethub) reached a recent low in 2014 of 11.82%. Therein we can easily witness the 10 percentage point difference in the realm of banking. Indeed the situation at the time of writing this book was even worse with creditcards.com reporting a 17.41% average interest rate on credit cards during a time when US interest rates moved to a giddy height of 2.5%..

The only word for this sort of spread between the wholesale price and the retail price in the modern world is egregious. Or rather it is more fair to say that the whole business of credit as provided by banks has simply failed to keep up with the modern digital micropayment world.

A simple comparison with capital markets can suffice. Head off to an exchange in any major financial centre today and you can trade debt instruments in interest rates or bonds for nickels and dimes. Likewise, the difference between buying and selling (or to some effect borrowing and lending) is a few basis points. That compares poorly with the friendly (sic) local bank branch, or even their groovy online interface through the web. The result could not be more stark.... Deposit money and the interest you receive (besides being the square root of almost nothing for much of the QE generation from the turn of this century) is a handy 10 percent or more away from what the same bank will offer to lend you money.

Think about that for a moment – 10 PERCENT! That's 1000 basis points... Before bankers claim they have been impugned at what I think is a fairly generous interpretation of the spread for the bank's hard pressed clients, remember the simple truth is the capital markets see transactions at sub a basis point on the world's exchanges. Likewise, opened to post deregulation competition, the cost of transacting most products on exchanges have collapsed by 90%+ during the past decade whereas the banking system is stuck with a simply decrepit model which is unable to cope with less than being thousands of times more expensive than the modern alternatives...

Of course the irony is that banks maintain their power not so much through money per se but by that piece of balance sheet leveraging whereby they dominate financial discussions. Banks have proven some of the most adept lobbyists in history. If only they could devote the same resources to, well, banking, they might not be in their current relatively dire straits! The ultimate banking racket is in fact lobbying – from these positions the banks practice an acute ability to influence all manner of activities in financial markets and assiduously cry wolf at any point in time when their monopolistic self-interest if not properly represented (i.e. steamrollered through to the banks' sublime benefit). The net result of this pure hypocrisy is some pretty ridiculous posturing by banks at the expense of perceived competition to their outpriced and outmoded monopoly.

Thus banks complain vociferously about the stock and derivatives exchanges essentially extorting money from them but the reality is that there is no clear correlation between the banks' own processes and how other financial intermediaries can build lasting businesses on fees of vastly lesser magnitude than the banks seek to extort at all times because they deem it their divine right. Too many banks have an approach to hypocrisy on the higher end of the camel needle threading zone of the belief defying scale

Thus modern digital bourses have a proven ability to make healthy profit margins with fractions of a basis point in total costs… All the while banks breezily ignore the world's digital future by expecting to garner a bid-offer spread of easily 1000 basis points or more for their core operation of lending money! Oh and they habitually complain that exchanges are ripping them off to boot on account of high profit margins from the micropayments levied by the bourses.

I write this not as a treatise to be added to the anti-capitalist leitmotiv for flogging bankers which remains in vogue in some 'liberal' circles. Ironically, if only the anti-bank squad bothered to analyse the core of banking itself, they would see that the world of banking is in fact on the verge of its own massive disintermediating moment. However I do support the notion of reigning in banks and indeed never again bailing out their definitively idiotic lending practices in extreme bubbles with a blank cheque. Protect depositors and maintain trust but let the charlatans go bust… Meanwhile build better links between banks and what they are supposed to do: finance business. Again that also requires some regulatory pragmatism.

The truth is that banks are slow, sclerotic, incompetent and largely customer oblivious. There are specialist arms of banks which may maintain that they are hugely customer sensitive such as private banks but actually said institutions seem to be more concerned in my experience with charging even higher fees to richer customers than really aiming to define good service per se. This is probably harsh on many reasonable banking franchises but the problem is that pretty much every bank in the world is currently uncompetitive from a pricing and standards perspective with the way the digital world is developing.

At this juncture, I can feel you will be in two minds, dear reader.

For a number of you, this all seems to be a reasonable response. Disintermediation is essentially understood by financial practitioners everywhere but most within financial markets are already too closely allied to the status quo that I suspect you will be either suspicious of, or traumatized by, the notion that after a strong run for the past 5 or 6 centuries and beyond, banks are now actually about to face a fundamental struggle for their survival.

On the other hand, a group of people may not be altogether surprised that the disintermediating process that is already attacking the print media, publishing generally, the music industry and many other areas, are in fact going to end up with banking following in their wake.

However, what is this brave new world that can be envisaged, if not, without banks, at least with banks less epcientral to the cohesion of finance?[2]

Ultimately, the digital world likes brief, simple transactions. Crisp instant settlement is encouraged, if not mandatory, as well. To that end, intermediaries are few and far between. The digital world likes reducing the layers in the millefeuille of intermediaries to the logical opposite of the layers comprising the millefeuille pastry first recorded by 17th century cookery writer François Pierre de la Varenne. The message hasn't changed since Capital Market Revolution!: If you can't add value to the food chain, then the chain will simply pass you by and compress itself to make the chain simpler and indeed, cheaper and faster. Even when you have a regulatory privilege – one which is genuinely exorbitant.

Ultimately, you could say that in some ways the core of commerce is simply returning to the origins of the bazaar. At the same time, it is only fair to note that platforms are popular as they create a core

---

2. There are those who could argue with reason that using the words "cohesion" and "banks" given the way they managed to self-immolate in the run up to 2008 is perhaps foolhardy.

basis for the development of trust. Within financial transactions, the trust issue is a key factor. Ironically, one of the things which I would contend will most promote the disintermediation of the banks is the fact that overall bankers have, not without reason, lost the trust of the population. For those who doubt this, bear in mind that as the US banking crisis was abating, an opinion poll in March 2012 showed that some 10% of customers in the UK and USA would be interested in banking with Apple, the computer giant. For existing users of Apple's ultra-cool technology, this percentage rose to a remarkable 43%![3]. Indeed when "Capital Market Revolution!" was first published in 1999 a lot of media was discussing how Microsoft were thinking about entering banking. At the time of finishing "Victory Or Death?" the media had moved on to unbridled excitement about Apple Credit Cards. (Despite this book being written on MacBooks Pro and Air, I must admit that while Microsoft Bank sounded like an interesting segue perhaps the passage of the years has dulled my being overly excited by an Apple credit card).

Ultimately, the one phrase you don't tend to overhear in supermarket queues is "oh I just love my bank, they are so efficient and good to me." It is rarer than Douglas Adams' gem of an observation "It can hardly be a coincidence that no language on Earth has ever produced the expression "as pretty as an airport." Indeed Adams (in "The Long Dark Tea-Time of the Soul") went on to observe "Some attain a degree of ugliness that can only be the result of a special effort." A phrase I feel could more than adequately surmise contemporary feelings about banks.

Meanwhile, banks themselves remain blissfully oblivious to this trend while trying to shoehorn greater fees out of the customer base for providing fewer services – and indeed ideally services online. That

3. http://www.reuters.com/article/2012/03/20/
   idUS106632+20-Mar-2012+PRN20120320

brings us back to that odd time I visited a branch of ING Bank in Poland and was charged for depositing cash.

Yes, once again you read that sentence correctly. Deposit cash in a bank and you have to pay for the service. Perhaps one of the reasons why Apple is so successful and regarded as better at banking than banks without even trying to provide such services is that Apple stores are a cornucopia of service with row upon row of gadgets laid out to be played with and tested. Presumably if ING Bank ran the Apple store, they would charge users for a demo. Goodness only knows what it would be like taking an iPad with a cracked screen to the Genius bar for service. On the other hand at least bankers would be happy at the recognition of their genius, even if a wealth of evidence can be garnered to suggest bank and genius goes together as appropriately as "pretty" and "airport." Then again we're back full circle. In 1999 at the peak of their influence, a company called Microsoft had been reported as discussing whether it wanted to buy a bank and try finance... Thus Apple may not solve the problems of finance and indeed nor may finance necessarily solve the problems of Apple's iPhone achieving some element of market saturation.

Ultimately, banks are desperate to push all their customers out of capital intensive branches and make them use online platforms. Leaving aside the sheer awfulness of many such platforms (and the fact that log in procedures are either so "secure" even the customers often cannot log in, or so user-oblivious that one wonders which planet the IT staff came from), the truth is that banks have signed their own death warrant through such activity.

Of course the banks will wail about such facets to business as Basel III which require banks to maintain higher capital but then again the only reason banks remain in the dog house of public opinion is that they have consistently behaved with all the decorum of Homer Simpson at an 'all you can eat' buffet and their lending policies were broadly dismally sheep-like as they sought to make money without any reasonable assessment of risk.

However, the saving grace is that by pushing customers online, then the banking industry is helping accelerate its own death as a centrepoint of capitalism. True, banks won't die out entirely and indeed they may even enjoy a resurgence in decades to come just as cinemas did when they discovered comfortable chairs and all manner of pyrotechnics. However, the simple fact is that the great, golden age of banks as the epicentre of capitalist interaction is headed towards bit part status as opposed to major league dominance. Banks can survive that have a specific well serviced niche. Massive department stores which claim to help everybody but truly serve nobody, not even their own staff and shareholders on occasion, face a much more challenging outlook.

Ironically, if we go back to the theory of Apple Bank (and I stress it is just a theoretical construct designed by opinion pollsters as an outright bank – for now...), then actually we can see that in reality, if Apple were going to do a bank, they presumably wouldn't be doing it the dull old conventional way. Oh, and I don't just mean Apple would give banking all manner of cool interfaces and interesting design. Rather, I mean that 'Apple Bank' (as opposed to the modest New York focussed entity Apple Bank), would undoubtedly do things differently and indeed, to that end, they have already provided the model through other services.

Yes, indeed folks, it's time to revisit that "D" word, the one which makes most of the population go "huh?" yet can reduce every broker, banker and middleman to a frothing wreck within a New York minute.[4]

In established capital markets, true the revolution has left a lot of middlemen intact and in many cases, exchanges and platforms

4. Johnny Carson: "it's the interval between a Manhattan traffic light turning green and the guy behind you honking his horn." Algo traders may find it easier to consider the construct an example of everyday low latency human interaction.

have so far fallen short of destroying certain intermediated oligopolies: I'm thinking of you, US Treasury bond market. That said, electronic bond market platforms finally appear to have crested some form of tipping point, at least if gushing headlines about the rise of electronic platforms are to be believed. Actually thee is a serious point here. 20 year veterans of the bond market electronification such as Lee Olesky CEO of Tradeweb clearly demonstrate how no market is immune to the Capital Market Revolution! – with a cornucopia of competing platforms from the likes of CME, ICE, MarketAxess and Nasdaq amongst many gradually eroding the old bond market oligopoly. At the same time, that process has been accelerated where banks have either lacked the capital to enter / maintain bond dealing (qv various Eastern European markets which emerged post Communism such as Poland and Russia. There bonds trade on the national stock exchanges).

In the world of music and publishing, Apple has done a great deal of disintermediating already. Take iTunes, that rather ubiquitous source of digital downloads for iPods and other music players. Interestingly the strength of iTunes has remained even in a world where the iPod itself has become outmoded. At the music level, costs have been compressed and record labels have lost their oligopoly power of distribution. In podcasts, the directory networks like iTunes essentially enable anybody anywhere to produce audio content for listeners across the world. True, it does mean some rather lovely record stores have disappeared but then again so have lots of fairly awful ones too. Likewise, games can be downloaded from the App store and indeed books can be digitally downloaded from Apple, Amazon or various other sources. The end result is much easier access to media for consumers, at a lower cost than was the case when we still bought solid state things like records, dvds, or cassettes.

Ultimately, banking may have moved online in many facets but it certainly isn't digital. Born Analogue it is just, well "Ba"...

…Banking has a long way to go until it gets the "Living Digital" component. Window dressing and listening to the soothing sounds of pliant consultants isn't going to cut through to the brave new world digital natives are building with the help of those born analogue folks who have made the transition.

Meanwhile digital entrepreneurs assessing opportunity in legacy markets, or seeking whole new swathes of profitable segment come in many strands. When assessing the likes of exchanges, a small but dedicated cohort spot opportunities within the micropayment arenas – a vast bulk of exchanges and market platforms have been established during the past decade precisely as exchange charges have been consistently shaved through competitive dynamics. At the same time, it has been hard to ignore the gaping chasm of de facto bid/offer spreads in banking and the opportunity provided. Where exchanges are within a fraction of a basis point – actually competitors are now discounting by bare nickels and dimes, in banking you have that juicy 1000 basis point (10 percentage points!) spread between where the bank borrows (your deposits) and where it lends (overdrafts, credit cards et al). At this point I ought to note that when it comes to secured lending like mortgages banks tend to 'only' charge a spread of about 150-200 basis points on their lending. It's better than the de facto 'Dick Turpin does banking factor' in the unsecured market but it makes little or no sense when it comes to analysis with, say corporate secured lending in bonds., It's still a vastly outmoded analogue process – with reams of paper at all stages and quasi-endless customer oblivious time wasting. Oh and don't even get me started on the ludicrous paperwork of mortgage lending… Albeit there is some relief at hand there as Intercontinental Exchange have been endeavouring to revamp a lot of mortgage paperwork through their 2018 acquisition of Mortgage Electronic Registration Systems and then the 2019 purchase of Simplifile.

It is hardly unsurprising given the above huge margins that where the banks have left behind a bid/offer opportunity through which we could fit a significant item of road haulage – probably an Australian double trailer road train. There has been little problem navigating a small tank or armoured vehicle onto the well manicured lawns of the banks. When you compare the 1000 basis point travesty of banking to the wonderful world of microlending – very small commoditised transactions with origins in the east, it is hardly surprising that many scent opportunities in the general banking sphere. Originally, microlending (which begat microbanking) was developed by the likes of Muhammad Yunus, the founder of Grameen Bank. Grameen pioneered microlending to some of the poorest people on earth – frequently women (they also tend to have better repayment records) – in places like Bangladesh where even borrowing a few dollars could help place them on a path to entrepreneurship and economic self-sufficiency. Of course the advantage to the original microlenders of operating in very poor nations such as India, Pakistan, Bangladesh and parts of Africa, was that staff could also be employed at very low wages (compared to the west). Therefore V1.0 microlending was not especially technology-centric. Rather it was essentially analogue involving face to face meetings with a form of syndication. These pioneering programmes had some interesting twists, such as helping create loans to groups of women to produce a peer group incentive not to default on loans. Even in microlending, there have therefore been some fascinating risk management innovations!

Bank in banking land, they suffer the first gen microlender problems as a result of being legacy institutions which significantly pre-date the Napoleonic wars. Take any industry from that era and the only survivors are artisanal, nothing that scaled... every other form of commerce has evolved enormously. Yet the bank exists as the same concept it always ways – some internal capital, buffered by a form of backing (emotional support blankets with cash under conditions) as well as the anti-competitive veil of a suitable licence hugely cosseted by often aloof central bankers who appear to mainstream investors and businesses to often have a curious demeanour. The difficulty here is banking remains hugely poorly structured to the modern world customer base – in essence the heart of the universal bank is just too large and flaccid to be viable in the future. This relates to every feasible process. The 1000 basis point comfort zone is not merely because of any risk factor in lending unsecured, it is also hugely governed by the number of internal processes within a bank itself. Now, to be fair, one area where banks have been somewhat unable to defend themselves from extra costs is in regulation. Albeit a slight streak of culpability sets in given that banks overall, like all corporate socialist blobs, often acquiesce to cumbersome, tricky processes of regulatory fiat in order to help maintain a de facto competitive advantage. Thus the EU is swarmed by bankers arguing over the minutiae of rules which are often little more than plain dumb impediments to a free flowing economy for all. The EU does not have a monopoly stranglehold on daft legislation but is most recent master oeuvre, MIFID II is a singularly asinine piece of over-engineered business prevention and cost expansion for clients masquerading as a coherent regulations which ought to have been strangled during its misguided gestation. However, there can be no doubt, banks struggle with a lot of the AML / KYC and other regulatory process they must undertake when some of it is fairly absurdly onerous for no great benefit.

At the same time here arises a key flaw in banking – the herd instinct. This banks all tend to adapt to whatever a clique deems safe or sensible and follow with gusto. The sovereign debt farago of the 1970's is a good example. Freed from the constraints of many currency restrictions and with the offshore dollar market growing (thanks in part to a Kennedy era withholding tax), banks lent money to governments on the fabulously reasonable premise that governments could not go bankrupt – ergo there was no risk!

Readers may wish to consider just how coherent this was as managing risk oriented thinking but then again holistic is, judging from past track record, not a big word in many bankers lexicons. "No," "No," "No" and occasionally yes are pretty common but beyond the binary ultimately securing your executive patch in the banking 'jobsworth' culture seems to be more important than long-term strategy. Thus major banks retain this longstanding problem of, at best, thinking through what they are doing from a limited mindset while a massive herd instinct restricts their ability to be countercyclical in any way as they generally take the easy money which invariably floats seamlessly into the next bubble at which stage the market explode and bankers get left with egg on their faces but essentially no other penalty for their failure applies. For as we know, in the modern epoch of shameless bankers they simply move on to collect their de facto government insurance policy and start looking for a new bubble. To describe this as a rotten ecosystem is a significant understatement. That governments of varying ideology to right and left rushed with aplomb to bail out the banks during the last downturn demonstrates either comprehensive capture by the banks' lobbyists or incoherence on the part of the contemporary political genus...or perhaps both.

Anyway without much thought apart from following whatever herd emerges, all too many banks prove invariably incapable of coherently managing through the cycle.There are clear exceptions of course. When bankers wish to think outside the box, they can deliver longstanding shareholder value without a government bailout. The Rietumu Banka in Latvia survived where most others failed, broadly because they didn't lend money to property developers in the crazed mid-2000's bubble with the alacrity of a demented drug addict.. Indeed Rietumu was the sole Latvian bank to record a profit in 2009 while most of its local competitors struggled with any measure of solvency. Banking can be safe but when government offers an automatic bailout to the badly managed (as opposed to safeguarding some element of citizens' deposits). Of course this is not a financial technology problem per se but a legacy case that banks crowd and the wisdom of crowds may have been much discussed by James Surowiecki and others but ultimately banks also suffer from the madness of mobs across the cycle thanks to their seemingly innate herd instinct. Cue I suppose calls for Artificial Intelligence in banks as the DNA based management form seems to be so poorly installed...

Structurally, banks do not tend to think through their obligations either before or after they take them on – despite a welter of paperwork being demanded which appears to tick a myriad of boxes but add little to human knowledge. Rather the system is more complex than merely a pooling of 'knowledge' within banks. The commercial banks operate in lockstep with the central banks and governments which means when the fire is raging they add a bit more kerosene while, when the economy is in a trough they are assiduously licking their wounds. You may prefer the fabulous Albert Edwards of Societe Generale analogy of pushing the heads of partygoers into the punchbowl then pulling the bowl away at a point after which a healthy non hungover end to the party can be achieved. Of course banks are good at brand marketing and efficient as we have discussed, at lobbying. However, at this point it is best to ignore the window dressing of innovation officers and accelerators,. In essence banks are so hardwired in their current ways of dealing, they are broadly unable to change – a pity as they do have a future, just not in the current form.

The historic concept of banking is gradually going to be usurped as the dominant provider of loans through technological development which is remarkably similar to the concepts of file sharing networks, and social networks. Indeed, the whole of the internet has become a broadly democratic system in terms of the peer to peer relationships that can exist in many different forms of interaction.

In banking, bank operations are already being transformed into a peer to peer environment where the banks will be increasingly disintermediated from their old fashioned principal and broker mix. That segmentation, the provision of "Chinese walls" as they are known in the business becomes easier in the P2P banking world.

True P2P lending has already suffered some crises – the Chinese market imploded during 2018 with a large aftershock. The Chinese authorities clamped down and those deemed to have been fraudulent received swingeing sentences. Overall this cycle was symptomatic of growth pains, not a problem inherent to the concept of cheap efficient centralised platforms enabling borrowing and lending between peers through a trusted network. The most precise advantage of a P2P lender is the ability to disintermediate the bank and for a modest fee allow borrowers and lenders to essentially meet somewhere in the middle of that gargantuan 1000 basis point spread. Thus borrowers have lower repayments while lenders (or depositors in legacy banking parlance) have a greater return on their savings. Win Win for the customers...one more nail in the banker coffin.

Prosper Mutual in the USA and Zopa in the UK have been amongst the market leaders for over a decade. While in hiatus in China, the P2P revolution is expanding rapidly across India and other countries throughout the world.

With a simple disintermediating structure – a platform that provides an open market for borrowers and lenders – the basis of P2P is easy to understand predicated in a model which can be defined in one very simple sentence:

"anybody can lend to anybody else directly without recourse to a middleman."

At the same time, the business of peer to peer lending has already created multiple different variations to the simple concept. Clearly the aim is to facilitate as much lending as possible and thus many twists are being applied to ensure greater security for borrowers and lenders alike. Various concepts of risk management have been aforethought in the brave new world where a form of social media collides with cash-sharing networks. It is still somewhat prototypical but it is making headway.

Some networks have imposed strict limits on how much can be lent to one individual by any other individual in effect creating syndicated lending on the micro scale. Equally, many have sought to work in specific sectors, for instance trade finance, as well as property. Some P2P platforms enable a hybrid of corporate capital and retail funding / borrowing. Hence P2P platforms, across all manner of borrowing / lending requirements can be corporate to individual, individual to corporate, corporate to corporate or any mix which best suits the needs of platform users.

At all times, borrowers in particular have been ascribed ratings of sorts, in relation to their activity and certain financial data. Clearly, anti-money laundering statute must be adhered to at all times alongside mitigating for theft risk et al. At the same time, whereas banks are stuck with conventional credit ratings, the P2P universe is just one of several areas where forms of credit rating calculation can be part of the borrowing / lending mix. Thus even data which may appear at first bland sources of financial data, such as social media streams are being deployed, by P2P platforms, cell phone companies and even insurers to get a better picture of the client… On a very simple basis, he (and it usually is a he) who spends a lot of time discussing pure speed on the open highways ought not to be surprised when insurers deem them a higher risk. Similarly social media can provide interesting analytical insights into how we claim to spend our money on bank forms as opposed to how it looks when digitised for Instagram, on a plate or elsewhere. Meanwhile, insurance products have begun to emerge to permit the lender to protect their loans, albeit clearly for a reduced return. Naturally a cornucopia of other products can be added to a P2P platform using the widely available hedging building blocks of futures and options from the major derivatives exchanges to enable all form of hedging given the outlook of interest rates from a particular borrower or lender too.

The core advantage in P2P lending is of course the "win win" which makes conventional banking a "lose lose" for all clients – the disintermediation of the middle bank means that borrowers and lenders can meet on much more favourable terms to each party. Splitting a vast 1000 basis point spread (or more) is naturally hugely attractive to borrower and lenders alike. A total "win win" for all and a huge boon to economic efficiency where the banks are costing borrowers and depositors alike with their inefficient intermediation. The core spread of legacy banking may be a handy little earner for the banks but frankly a disaster for both borrowers and savers. Given that so many banks, despite being gifted a 1000 basis point spread are still worryingly closer to insolvency than balance sheet solidity a decade after the 2008 financial crisis only adds insult to consumer injury.

Therefore, P2P lending creates a model where borrowers and lenders (depending on the nature of loan, loan term, credit condition of the borrower etc) will fall closer to the mid-point between deposit and borrowing rates at a bank. In other words, instead of receiving 0.5% on deposit and paying 10% or more to borrow, the likely mid-point for a P2P transaction (ceteris paribus) is likely to be around 5-6%.

At this stage, things start to look a bit tricky for banks as their huge and costly infrastructure is de facto obsolete. Who needs hundreds of loan staff to coordinate borrowings and payments when citizens can be free to lend and borrow amongst themselves? This is of course a tricky concept for bankers who maintain an outsized belief that somehow they are a vital epicentre to commerce. In reality they are broadly reviled as part of the problem with financing business, not the solution, grudgingly used by businesses who simply need access to the financial system to pay wages, overheads and receive money. It is also difficult for regulators who have an equally misplaced old line belief that banks are either socially or financially required for a market based economy. The blunt truth is neither precept is true but clearly regulators are the ultimate anti-Schumpeterians when it comes to doing anything which will endanger their own generously provisioned government pensions and salary packages.

True, banks will still be somewhat relevant for one reason: leverage. The fractional reserve banking system permits banks to lend one dollar of deposits many times over. This makes for a tricky situation in terms of expanding money supply and indeed impacts the role of government. In future, the economy might not be so easy to leverage as it has been for governments in the post World War 2 era. That may make growth more difficult but then again it might also reduce some of the more extreme booms and busts in the cycle too. The pure macro economic ramifications of peer to peer lending I will leave for another time. That said, it is not difficult to see how leverage may be added to the system with a whole new fractional reserve system where some banks may remain more as proprietary capital risk traders (akin to hedge funds) injecting leveraged funds into the P2P lending market in some way or other. This is an important economic point. A decade ago I was disparaged by a particularly corpulent central banker at a private conference for noting that by somewhere around 2020 P2P banking would be making significant inroads into the core of bank lending. This was a preposterous notion to the economist in question whose mind numbing lack of intellectual curiosity was clearly the result of his brain being reduced to a kind of macro-ego.

Had the discussion been allowed to continue rather than being haughtily dismissed, I would have asked the key question on just how we can continue to evolve our fractional reserve based financial system when P2P deposits are essentially not going to scale, at least at domestic level. I can see ways forward – there are clearly opportunities for institutions to concentrate on lending via P2P while using the rights of banks to borrow on the money market without maintaining the pre-Dickensian trappings of the legacy banking industry. Hedge funds or other vehicles may create leverage from derivatives or using some modern hybrid of borrowing short to lend long but in the end somebody somewhere has to have collateral to lend the money P2P. This creates a huge economic issue which could ultimately see consumers empowered as higher yielding 'depositer/lenders' and a more efficient main street thanks to lower borrowing costs but overall the economy is no longer so fiscally leveraged. Of course the biggest issue here will come from Central Bankers who in the modern era have become the agents of leverage – particularly with increasingly desperate attempts to make the economy grow despite sclerotic regulation such as Quantitative Easing. There needs to be a significant rebalancing away from a certain arrogant caste of global central bankers towards a more sound money outlook before the true nature of P2P can be unleashed and the money supply according tweaked (as opposed to being outright debased) to allow for the new era of money...

...Oh and of course then we are touching upon the whole issue of cryptocurrency where a huge disintermediating force is upon the central banking and all of its ecosystem... Moreover, think back to Capital Market Revolution! where I discussed the future of money based on electronic values with lots of different asset underpinnings... Thanks to blockchain enablement, the possibility remains to move further to disintermediate central bankers from money by creating more and more perfectly fungible, liquid assets that are not manipulated by central bank or government whim... Of course those exquisitely distributed ledgers are wonderful for correlating money supply with the currency which exists but it causes a problem with introducing credit into the system...

The key facet to bear in mind is that where P2P lending is reformulating the core structure of borrowing and lending, so too it will therefore have a huge knock-on effect. These impacts will force banks to entirely restructure what operations they can hold on to. Sadly for the banks, with customer contempt for their rather lousy concepts of service growing all the time, it will prove difficult to maintain customer loyalty in the long-term as clients have become used to shoddy treatment, if not rampant incompetence from the banks themselves.

Whether you have been stranded by the whim of HSBC – whose Premier rollout became a rapid retreat in various territories after 2008, the simple problem remains that banks driven by quarterly profit targets make lousy bedfellows for those with longer perspectives, retail or corporate whereas banks manage to drive ineffective short-term agendas after seeming to create great strategic plans. The problem is they rarely stick to their strategic plans and HSBC alone seems to have gone through several CEOs just during the recent gestation of this book. Banks post 2008 began to sign their own death warrants with their rapid withdrawals of service and disappearance from key markets with a paucity of notice, assistance or even remorse at their actions. This was in the wake of the legacy banker' hubristic meltdown in the post 2008 property bubble which was at least partially expanded thanks to their egos being inflated by politicians who deluded themselves they had demolished the economic cycle (QV former Finance Minister and PM Gordon Brown, who inflicted severe long-term damage on the UK's indebtedness). Back at HSBC when they withdrew their Premier service in territories as diverse as Monaco, Poland and Russia, staff were left exposed to angry customers through no fault of their own – and that was only the start of the great branch retrenchment exercise. Thus despite their incredibly privileged monopoly over a 1000 basis point spread in their core business, banks have further drained customer loyalty even without recourse to being left behind technologically. Thus short termist management concentrates on the art of their career survival and ego burnishing. For most modern bankers, coherence is broadly ignored and creativity is a greater liability than an incomprehensible multi-clause Credit Default Swap in the eye of a liquidity crisis. None of this engenders customer loyalty but it remains a clear memory amongst all those who have been let down by their banking service (sic) provider (sic). A thousand banks have emulated the cackhanded management of HSBC in some branch, nation or region. HSBC perhaps stands out as it has managed through all manner of management crises to upset clients pretty much right across the globe. It amounts to globalisation of a sort but not really a sound approach to long-term survival methinks.

Back to the competing P2P structures. As a means to use

micropayments and even microloans, the P2P lending revolution upends banking and delivers a vast slug of efficiency to consumers and businesses alike that banks are simply unable to compete with given their sclerotic model bonded to a 1000 basis point model. The difficulty is not the idea of shaving the borrowing / lending margin down, the stark reality is bankers resemble something akin to the water wheels they financed in the 18th century and not even the steam power they financed 100 years later. This is at a time when society is on the cusp of fusion power...

At the same time bankers with their love of the herd, are simply unable to break away from time honoured modes of thinking and operating as the management culture prefers spineless continuation as opposed to genuine innovation. That's before the regulatory blob places ever more restrictions on cohesive service provision. Lipgloss accelerators and innovation hipster staffers aside, the simple fact is banks are paralysed with the idea of moving away from their old means of credit calculation and adding new tools that may make them more efficient. This is just one area where banks have relegated themselves to massive cost cutting behemoths, obsessed with cutting staff and branches while not actually comprehending how to build business – let alone relations with clients. Technology is powering this crisis for the bankers but the bankers have only themselves to blame for their dismally short-term career centric cowardice in responding to this brave new world.

Therefore we arrive at the big question for banks: Given their 1000 basis point advantage in their core business, how can they retain financial dominance when they are expensive, perverse, customer oblivious and even charge customers for having the temerity to use the historical traditional kind of physical cash.

Spoiler alert: They don't.

5. The Peak of Banker Power

"When money is lent on a contract to receive not only the principal sum again, but also an increase by way of compensation for the use, the increase is called interest by those who think it lawful, and usury by those who do not."

William Blackstone's Commentaries on the Laws of England, 1765.

It's fair to say Luca de Pacioli had an eye for beauty. Albeit his beauty was based around maths more than the pure subjectivity which can encroach much of the painted world. Pacioli remains a polymath poster boy from the renaissance era, thanks to his metier delivering remarkably prolific precis' of learning across a series of subjects centred around mathematics. A Franciscan friar, he was a friend and collaborator of Leonardo Da Vinci from 1497 to 1506 during which time Da Vinci illustrated Pacioli's study in mathematics and the geometry of art "The Divine Proportion" which was published in 1509 a decade after completion circa 1498. In historical terms, the two perhaps made slightly curious companions, living together for a while and also travelling / working concurrently around Italy after they hastily left Milan when it was invaded. Art historians believe Pacioli may have helped influence the proportions in Da Vinci's 1498 depiction of the Last Supper. Pacioli was highly adept at compiling research and regurgitating it in palatable formats. Thus the friar delivered near encyclopedic summaries of the knowledge accrued in particular areas at the time. Amongst his other works he surmised contemporary mathematical knowledge in his 1494 book "Summa de arithmetica, geometrica, proportioni et proportionalita." This tome was also significant – and here it intersects neatly with this tome's narrative – in discussing a summary of the method of accounts used by Venetian merchants during the Italian Renaissance. This codified practice was titled double entry book keeping. At the time it represented a quantum leap forward in the development of business accounting. Pacioli has had a good run from history in this regard as many refer to him as the "Father of Accounting."

The system that Pacioli published is a very closely correlated with the basis of accounting we know today. Amongst the wisdom he dispensed: Pacioli was eager to note that no merchant should sleep at night until their debits equaled their credits for example. There was even some content devoted to the ethics of accounting too.

Given that Pacioli was an excellent chronicler of many things – one of his early maths books delved into Fibonacci-series related issues (first published by Leonardo of Pisa in the Liber Abaci of 1202 AD for instance) there is cause to question whether his thesis on accounting might be all his own work, as it were, or merely a regurgitation of existing thinking, as was his talented wont. Indeed some decades earlier, on the eastern side of the Adriatic in the magnificent walled city of Ragusa (now Dubrovnik) Benedikt Kotruljević had been born in 1416. Benedetto Cotrugli (as he is known in Italian) became an accomplished Ragusan merchant, economist, scientist, and humanist. Furthermore as a diplomat, he spent some 15 years in the Court of Naples, where he would die in the city of Aquila in 1469, when Pacioli (born circa 1447) was still a young man.

Kotruljević wrote "Della Mercatura e Del Mercante Perfetto," a book completed in 1458 albeit the oldest version on record dates from 1475. That said it was not published until 1573 in Venice, in a significantly revised and abridged edition. Demonstrating a rare instance of the Anglosphere being in arrears of mercantile thought, the first English language edition only appeared (as "The Book of the Art of Trade") in 2017. Making up for the delay, Harvard University Press at least wielded a selection of historian heavyweights such as Niall Ferguson contributing to this edition!

It is unsurprising that so many modern day experts weighed in to assess his masterwork. For Cotrugli's manuscript is about much more than just bookkeeping. Indeed Cotrugli appears to have been a somewhat reluctant merchant, called from his studies at the university of Bologna to join the family business. This may be reflected in the deep consideration of his book which is in essence the first how-to business manual. The Book of the Art of Trade is divided into 4 separate volumes. The first is devoted to the origin, form and essence of being a merchant. The second looks at the merchant's religious commitment. Herein Cotrugli espouses a lot of sound CSR that would be appreciated by ethical investors today. Similar sentiments are maintained in the third volume which is related to moral virtues and policies. Then the fourth section is devoted to the administration of the merchant's home, family and his economic affairs. Cotrugli advises merchants to be leaders who are charitable, ethical and treat people fairly. He is keen to ensure merchants are modest and look for the right qualities in their wife (diversity wasn't big in 1458, so this book is predicated men working and women focussed on domesticity). His advice to be selective in deals which I quoted at the start of the previous chapter has a timeless quality to it, although views may differ on Cotrguli's advice to retire at 50... alas the merchant from Ragusa himself only lived to be 53 albeit that was a significant improvement on the life expectancy of about 35 in the 15th century.

Interestingly the earliest known surviving manuscript of the Cotrugli's mercantile treatise is located in the National Library of Malta, a bare few minutes walk from my current home in Valletta. More interesting still in the history of double entry book keeping, the same library collection housed a book which further unlocks the mystery of just who was originally codifying what became the quantum leap in accounting with debits to the left and credits to the right. For Cotrugli gives a brief review of required bookkeeping for merchants but it is hardly a full course. That it transpires was found in a manuscript which lay cared for but somewhat neglected –

broadly unread for a couple of centuries in the august surroundings of the National Library of Malta. It was not merely physically proximate to Cotrugli's book, this manuscript was ultimately bound to "The Book of the Art of Trade" by an early accounting student. That treatise, even missing some pages, turns out to have been the 'real deal' when it comes to being an actual unifying text, teaching the first codified accounting practice which was by then becoming standard practice across the Italian speaking territories. It is the transitional fossil of early accounting which delivers the missing link in the arc which curves through Kotruljevic, Pacioli and all the way to the 'big four.'

Book keeping was to a large degree localised in the late 1400s with different standards in different city states and territories across the Italian speaking lands where the western world's major commercial centres were to be found. Accounting was learnt through apprenticeship as opposed to formal study. The concept of double entry probably began emerging in 13th century Florence if not earlier, at the time when the Hindu-Arabic number system was first finding its way into books such as Leonardo of Pisa's Liber Abaci (1202) which as I noted above, Pacioli had also discussed in his work.

Intriguingly there is also evidence that during the Goryeo dynasty (918-1232) when Kaeson was a major commercial centre, the Korea had developed a form of double entry system: the Four-element bookkeeping system during the 11th or 12th century.

The earliest remaining accounting records following the double-entry system in Europe come from the pen of the Florentine merchant Amatino Manucci. Manucci was employed by the Giovannino Farolfi & Company, a firm of Florentine merchants headquartered in Nîmes who acted as moneylenders with their most important customer being the Archbishop of Arles. The Farolfi firm ledger of 1299-1300 displays clear evidence of full double-entry bookkeeping albeit an incomplete record of the accounts has survived. Meanwhile, the earliest complete record of a double entry system in Europe dates to the accounts of the Republic of Genoa in

1340. The "Messari" (Treasurer's) accounts contain journalised debits and credits with balances carried forward from the previous year. That system would attain widespread adoption amongst bankers and merchants in Florence, Genoa, Venice and Lubeck by the end of the 15th century.

The breakthrough in standardised double entry book keeping came at the start of the 15th century. Previously only two books were used for accounts, a memorandum book and a ledger. Thus control could be exerted over debtors and creditors. However, there was not much interest in calculating profit or wealth. Around 1408, the introduction of the Journal created what nowadays may be breathlessly termed 'a paradigm shift.' The core leap involved the deployment of a journal which delivered chronology to the entries therein. In other words, time and it's bedfellow duration, leapt into the consciousness in a fashion that previously had been much more vague. Thereafter a clear accounting narrative was created, quite contrary to the rather disparate muddle of figures in different places which had prevailed, where multiple entries were scattered across many pages in a ledger. The journal also led to a form of standardisation of approach. Moreover with the journal at the epicentre of the new book keeping methodology, the whole process of accounting became much easier to teach. Teaching (as opposed to explaining) is something which neither the volumes by Pacioli or Cotrugli ostensibly do. Explain: yes. Actually go through the nitty gritty of how to create your accounts, they do not. At this juncture in search of the textbook, another Ragusan merchant enters the narrative:

Marino de Raphaeli, like Cotrugli, hailed from Dubrovnik. In 1475 he accepted a commission to teach double entry bookkeeping to Zuan de Domenego, who was a member of the extended family of one of the twelve original noble houses of Venice. First de Raphaeli travelled to Naples to make a copy of Benedetto Cotrugli's manuscript of The Book of the Art of Trade. Then he went to the

Venetian Republic where he proceeded to teach his student by dictation.

His student would ultimately be given de Raphaeli's manuscript copy of the Cotrugli book which de Domenego bound along with his own notes as dictated by de Raphaeli. The resulting number sequenced folio became one bound volume. This volume itself reached Malta sometime before 1747 and effectively languished in sunny obscurity in the southern Mediterranean. The significance of the De Raphaeli / de Domenego folio only became transparently apparent in July 2013 when Scottish university professor Dr Alan Sangster spent three weeks in Malta examining the historical tome. As Dr Sangster notes "De Raphaeli is very much at the beginning of this process and it is to him and his contemporaries rather than to Pacioli that we should look for the catalyst that led to the development of accounting into the form we know it today."

Thus the history of double entry keeping steered its way from De Raphaeli's rigorous course driven by the appendix to Cotrugli's "Book of the Art of Trade" and eventually popularised by the polyglot precis master Pacioli.

Great inventions in the public mind are generally viewed as those remarkable feats of engineering or other entirely physical objects which of course tend to be more photogenic (and certainly more arresting in oils) than mere shufflings of numbers. Isambard Kingdom Brunel's remarkable bridges, or Karl Benz's automobile excite vastly more interest than, well, a few notebooks scribbled full of numerals, no matter how arresting their tabular positioning may render them. Yet the invention of coherent accounting in the form of double entry book keeping vastly changed the world and its growth trajectory. Mill owners had to wait a few centuries for the industrial revolution to catch up to the financial innovation enabled by Italian renaissance bookkeeping but adding the journal along with other accounting books created a data revolution equivalent to the development of the personal computer almost 600 years later. Accounting enabled the organisation of vast quantities of financial data into these journals, in a a simple, legible and coherent narrative, with the calendar at its core. From these journals companies could produce a balance sheet as well as income statements and thus coherently assess the success and value of their business endeavours. Balance sheets provided the clarity of assets and debts and thus changes in owners' equity. Income statements enabling the understanding of profit and loss could demonstrate changes in profits and of course that affected equity. Suddenly a holistic understanding of commerce was feasible. Indeed this rapidly led to the greater adoption of fascinating early financial instruments. The bill of exchange was a genius invention which enabled merchandise to be bought overseas using a note which could be converted into specie with a local banker. These bills effectively incorporated an interest rate component embedded in the foreign exchange rate thus avoiding the churches standing against usury.

However as Alex Mayyasi notes[1]

"In 1462, Franciscan monks in Italy created the first non-profit pawnshops or monti di pietà ('banks of piety'), which went on to spread across Europe. The idea was to be like a Grameen Bank in Renaissance Italy – a lender of last resort, displacing loan sharks who extorted desperate borrowers. The Pope went on to approve ever more kinds of financial instruments, until lending with interest was effectively allowed."

The ultimate de facto deregulation of money lending thus enabled a massive financial revolution. The reformation and the development of protestant churches with a disregard for forbidding usury further accelerated the process of interest rates being charged on debts.

However for lending to grow, this required the development of accounting. As Steve Mariotti notes: "Out of the income statement

1. https://aeon.co/essays/how-did-usury-stop-being-a-sin-and-become-respectable-finance

came the intellectual miracle of the return on investment (ROI) which allowed investors to compare investments mathematically with the simple ROI formula and soon after, the business community started to add risk to the analysis which was another game changer.")[2]

As accounting enabled relative risk analysis, the whole field of risk and reward opened up in a new and scientific fashion. Thus we arrived at the fundamental equation of business value, as fundamental as E=MC2 Assets = Liabilities + Shareholders' Equity. That led to a value explosion as assets could be traded for their reasonable data-derived value and underpinned with debt at a sensible level according to their ability to fund repayment. Like all great financial revolutions, the delivery of accounting enabled economic growth which in turn enabled greater prosperity, lifting millions from poverty.

When accounting and debt were wedded of course a whole new paradigm in the economy was enabled and that required one key third actor, the bank.

Banking has of course much older roots than the invention of accounting and basic lending has taken place for millennia. The temple of Artemis at Ephesus was in its prime, the largest depositary in Asia (it was located around 75 kms from the modern port city of Izmir). This was a good example of a depository where gold and assets could be held against loans, often based on future crops. In Ancient Greece the rudiments of a banking system were gradually born. Xenophon has been credited by various historians as delivering the original organisational concept equivalent to a joint-stock bank in "On Revenues" which was written circa 353 BC.

However the modern banking entity was born, in medieval and early renaissance Italy, in northern city states such as Florence,

<hr>

2. https://www.huffingtonpost.com/steve-mariotti/so-who-invented-double-en_b_3588941.html)

Genoa and Venice. Initially the entities were "merchant banks" driven by the grain trade. Jews fleeing persecution in Spain brought the understanding of the silk roads from the middle and far east. Their skillset in financing long sea voyages was deployed to finance general trade and particularly grain production. As Jews were unable to own property in Italy, they set up their stalls for finance in the general markets and trading piazzas in Lombardy. The Jewish benches were invariably busy as they could lend money whereas Roman Catholics were precluded from usury by religious restrictions. Thus Jews engaged in the risky practice of lending at high interest rates in crop development, securing their loans against the eventual sale of the grains at market. Soon some of the merchant lenders began trading the grain debt itself instead of the grain.

Indeed Jewish traders became an early form of 'one stop shop' with forms of credit financing and underwriting / insurance functions which enabled the farmer to perform a full cycle from cultivation through seeding, growing, weeding and harvesting his crop. During the process, the Italian word for a bench counter "banca" became the term for a bank itself, while notes holding deposits for settlement of grain were "billette" from which originated the bill of exchange.

Banking clearly gained considerable developmental vigour as the Roman Catholic church relaxed its positions on usury in the early phase of double entry book keeping, even before the Templars and Hospitalliers for instance used their network of knights to act as bankers to King Henry II of England for instance. Indeed the earliest known foreign exchange contract dates back to 1156 when two brothers borrowed 115 Genoese pounds with settlement in Constantinople of 460 Bezants a month after their arrival in that city. Foreign exchange contracts grew rapidly as their profits were seen as a trading differential and not usury per se so did not infringe on canon law.

From these medieval origins through the renaissance, the crop-centric business of moneylending accelerated into a more modern banking industry when the widespread deployment of the double entry book keeping system enabled bankers to have a much clearer understanding of not merely their risks and potential rewards but also the value of assets they were lending against. From here it was equally not difficult to discern which loans were proving most profitable enabling a fledgling activity of financial analysis. As the economy expanded and the horizons of trade themselves moved significantly, diversification was feasible through looking at different types of risk – loans against trade, grains or voyages of exploration. Moreover banking was revolutionised as more forms of transactional instrument were created... The adoption of the bill of exchange became a key aspect to banking, allowing merchants to travel long distances without the impediment of carrying weighty bullion, grain certificates and bills of exchange establishing their own niches for trading separate to their pure trade function, banking grew rapidly.

With the growth of accounting, the expansion of money and the extension of trade, the world itself essentially expanded thanks to the development of cartography and later tools such as the sextant enabled better navigation. Thus the banking industry became an epicentre of commerce that helped power humankind into the industrial age, through the first era of mass transportation and into the jet era. Thus the double entry book keeping system changed the world and launched an opportunity for a new economic growth utterly unprecedented in history.

The bank unleashed an unprecedented growth in finance and became the benchmark institution linked to economic growth. From the era when a dose of leeches was the height of pharmaceutical innovation to the dawn of the biotechnology era, the bank has reigned supreme financing the agricultural economy, maritime exploration, the industrial revolution, countless wars and all manners of infrastructure, through to individual purchase of property, cars and consumer goods.

Until now.

True, banks still have some form of (I would argue diminishing) social cachet. They retain remarkable political leverage and their position in the regulatory nexus is at best, protected, at worst a hugely detrimental conflict of interest. Twenty years ago in "Capital Market Revolution!" I was struggling to see what their route forward would be. Nowadays that pathway looks to be one of a long drawn out decline.

At this stage of the narrative it is useful to segue into the history of innovations. Most vitally, there is always a clear lag between the arrival of a 'new new' thing in embryonic form all the way to mass market adoption. Cycles of innovation can be seen as two separate things. On the one side there is the actual innovation itself and how it develops. Meanwhile on the other side, we have the 'hype cycle.' There is no better term for the latter – it is what starts as a semblance of crazed ravings from the sleep deprived eccentrics who often build the new new things...and carries on to a broad range of early believers all the way through to a group who indeed can only be reasonably termed, snake oil salesmen. The first major phase of the cryptocurrency hype cycle for instance ended during 2018. While the price of Bitcoin kept dropping from its epic high of $19,783.21 on December 17, there was an ongoing crazed cycle of hype as amazing incredible revolutions were promised and ultimately delivery was not quite so marked. As with all hype cycles, investment processes, led by coin offerings such as ICOs resulted in huge amounts of money being raised while of course, as always, huge numbers of charlatans, con men and other dubious actors often pocketed the cash and didn't deliver, all, or occasionally, any, of the services they offered.

Looking back at previous hype cycles, we can see how, for instance in the dotcom bubble at the turn of the century, there were amazing processes which were being promised in 1999 but that world of a nascent embryonic Google et al actually showed up the limitations of the early software.[3] Like so many innovation cycles, the products required a lot of customisation and were thus not especially customer friendly. Of course a key reason for this was the simple infrastructure behind the web of 1999. As the dotcom bubble drove a tech recession in the early years of the new millennium, the web 2.0 was under development.

So much for the early cycle and the growth of innovation. When we look to the longer term, just as it is darkest before the dawn, so too anything at its peak looks simply unassailable. Yet while the peak can be extended for many years in a major cycle, the simple truth is the only way from a peak is down....

At the same time, when something reaches its peak the concept of it being in decline may seem anathema. At that stage the process appears so embedded in the process of everyday life that it is viewed as bizarre to believe it might ever be surpassed. Peak points are always fascinating because either a mania has gained popular hold (tulips to dotcom) or the established 'wisdom' of the crowd simply cannot fathom how there is something different ahead...

Now when it comes to banking, we also approach a societal taboo – the money issue. Thus banks have managed for centuries to weave a certain mysticism about their magnificence and of course their probity and safety. Of course the mask slips occasionally – banking crises include Overend Gurney, Herstatt, Lehman Brothers to name but three from the past 150 years alone. Even the world's oldest surviving bank Monte Paschi di Siena ran into financial difficulties in recent years having traded since March 4 1472, through dozens of sieges and wars, two of them full scale global conflicts.

The ego of the banking system is evident throughout its claims of history, of being at the epicentre of so much that has happened

3. footnote for millennials here - believe it or not there was a functioning global interweb thingie without either Facebook or Google, Instagram or Snapchat

and of course in the iconic architecture banks prefer. The classical Georgian columns still prevalent in many bank HQs have given way to stunning skyscrapers but the message is always the same: somebody occupying this much prime real estate is clearly safe, secure and going to be around forever. This logic does not always stand up to an economic test.

The problem with the architectural sense of purpose as longevity concept is that the great pyramids of Gizeh are still around fulfilling a very secondary purpose to their original construction (tourism as opposed to 7 star tomb) but ancient Egyptians seem to be in much less supply and their emperors are few and far between apart from amongst those hardy souls who believe in reincarnation.

Meanwhile 'traditional' banking has been in decline for some time. The epicentre of banking tradition "borrow short, lend long" was noticeably in decline when Franklin R Edwards & Frederic S. Mishkin (1994) wrote their paper on "The Decline of Traditional Banking"[4] noting how bank lending as a proportion of US commercial lending had declined from around 36% in 1974 to 22% by 1993. In essence the first waves of new financial products driven by the Nixon era deregulation ate into the traditional banks' customer base. Thus in one sense some savers opted for money market mutual funds and other deposit schemes operated by asset managers. At the same time the capital markets were growing and for many corporations it became vastly more efficient to borrow directly – disintermediating the banks from the whole process. Thus corporations began to issue more bills, bonds and commercial paper. Of course this is before we even begin to consider the impact of derivatives...for the move from the analogue world of traditional banking to the leap to the digital

4. *Full title: "The Decline of Traditional Banking Implications for Financial Stability and Regulatory Policy" https://www.researchgate.net/publication/46567205_The_Decline_of_Traditional_Banking_Implications_for_Financial_Stability_and_Regulatory_Policy

world of three dimensional derivatives is a constant stream running through the Capital Market Revolution! itself. Bankers long saw the derivatives market as something they had some form of exclusive monopolists right to distribute to their excessively profitable benefit. Unfortunately the bankers' naive faith in their own balance sheet sanctity, while rescued short term by a panicked cadre of politicians in 2008. Nowadays, banker power in derivatives is mostly only maintained as a result of regulatory inaction to fully push the brave new world built on the back of the 2009 Pittsburgh G20 conference when the banks had inelegantly managed to force down the ceiling of the citadel of finance.

By the time we had reached that point in the 2000's, an unholy trinity of idiocy had propelled the world's economy away from the nadir of 2001. Unfortunately banks over inflated a remarkable credit boom apparently lending to more or less anybody apart from those who could actually repay. The hyperleverage of the banking system led to a hideous market collapse and the coordinated life-boating of most banks and far too many bankers who were responsible for the original bust.

The actual causes and effects of the 2007 banking crisis are not the key factor. Rather the major element is that the 2007 market top represented the peak of the bank. The zenith of the banker has broadly been missed because of several reasons. For one thing it is a very early call and historians are unlikely to rush in behind me on a circa 600 year call until they see a fair bit more history to back up the assertion. Overall supercycle peaks are not something many notice so swiftly and the current media cycle is much more one at the shortest of scales as opposed to having the perspective to step back to look at a multi-century move... Besides, given their strong addiction to branding making banks heavy advertisers, the dead tree press will struggle to rapidly endorse anything which further endangers their shrinking advertising revenue pile. Thus the media may be as eager to slap down as a mere piffle of bad credit as opposed to the prevailing trend of "Capital Market Revolution!" At the same time, looking at the bigger picture, what else has survived from the era when De Rafaeli, Cotrugli and Pacioli were codifying double entry book keeping and thus propelling the 'traditional banking' era which peaked in 2007? Banking has done remarkably well surviving this long.

To spot 2007 as the peak of this 500+ year mega cycle from the Medici to modernity first requires a lot of obscuring data to be delicately scraped away, albeit most of these layers are in themselves evidence of the peak. For one thing, of course, there was the macroeconomy. Banks had lent with the vigour of those demented with glee at the prospect of endless increases in property values going hand in hand with their expenses. At the same time, we had a peak respect for bankers... That the pygmy political classes foolishly bailed out the old economy at this juncture is not surprising – the issue though is that the evidence of the decline in banker power had been apparent since at least the 1990's as economists such as Edwards and Mischkin were pointing out almost a quarter of a century earlier in the early 1990's. Nevertheless, 2007 was the peak in banking power. The turndown marked an inelegant slide from a sensational summit but somewhere along the line the property market had been bolstered to simply ludicrous valuations on various continents.

That said, it is not the cycles of property or emerging markets issues which ultimately caused the banks to peak out – nor was it the delivery of increasingly complex derivatives that uniquely marked the top. These were symptoms of a sort but not the fundamentals undermining the future of banker power. Rather, the fundamental problem was the march of technology itself which delivered a hammer blow across every aspect of the analogue banking industry. Moreover, like so many industries convinced of their own invincibility, banks and bankers have had a paucity of perspective about reaching the peak, let alone slipping off the other side of it into the long deep decline towards widespread redundancy.

For banks were in a funk by 2009 as they were pinned to their regulatory powers of exorbitant privilege. Simultaneously, the power of technology was encroaching on their once hallowed mopopolies. The technology that enables banks to cut costs essentially enables a whole new raft of competitors at every level and in every element of the department store which is a conventional retail bank. P2P processes are attacking the citadel of lending. Payment Service Processors (PSPs) are corralling the cash into their accounts where, at best, it can be a deposit clutch to the banking sector but no longer gives the banks the same flexibility. The cash is itself likely to flow through many payment networks which cost a fraction of the old lumbering systems where the banks had all manner of haircuts and elegant delays built in to cosset their financial position. Where they do investment, the brokerage fees are wafer thin and the returns in investment banking are proving more difficult as clients are cynical of an entitled status quo. Issuers are often seeking their own listing arrangements as they see little value in paying 7% to an investment bank for a road show not altogether unlike one long real estate open house, albeit with more time in a private jet. On the bond market, the capital required needs to be elsewhere as banks continue to patch the holes left behind from their previous lending eccentricities... In essence banks now look like King Kong at the denouement of the classic movie – a huge hulking creature angrily scrabbling at the attackers which surround it as it stands marooned in an untenable position.

So 2007 marked the peak of the market for banks. It was the end of an era and it's all downhill from here. Apologies...before we get to the end of this cliche-ridden paragraph, bear in mind one thing: we may be past the summit of banker power but the death of the bank is seriously over-estimated. That said what banks may end up doing is a whole new discourse for later. However in the meanwhile, let's appreciate just what being at the peak of the cycle means for banks. This isn't going to be a drop from the peak akin to Wil E Coyote finding himself up against the forces of gravity while holding the Acme anvil in a Looney Tunes cartoon. Indeed, this won't even resemble a fast hanglider back to a base camp somewhere in the 15th century. Rather this cycle will take a long time to play out. By long time we're likely talking at least the better part of a century, maybe more. That said the decline in banking power will be obvious soon (if it is not already – after all this author functions easily in Malta without a local bank account).

Banks rely on the huge overhang of their regulatory monopoly, their proximity to government and their perceived status to exploit the position. Thus they won't be sinking like the Titanic. As a vague comparative look at radio – the television apparently obliterated that after the second world war yet radio survived and thrived for many reasons. Even today the podcast era, in which I play a modest production role, is driving new radio stations (take the excellent niche global lifestyle channel Monocle 24 for instance) to produce ever more creative content, while separately YouTube and Vimeo revolutionize the world of television away from the quaint notion that programmes happen at a specific time on a particular fixed channel. The media is being distributed, the way we engage with money is being distributed too – and that will be detrimental to all banks which behave as if the status quo of, say 2005 remains.

However, make no mistake, the world moved on its axis in one clear sense when the doors of Lehman Brothers closed in 2008 and a multitude of banks required rescue. We don't need to rake over the coals of what was part criminal conspiracy and very much a triumph of moronic groupthink / linear thinking without recourse to logic where oversight clearly failed, in part aided by government forces believing they could keep the party going for just a few more years...

Of course, the 'enlightened' view is that could never happen again. This is mostly said by the sort of people who dismissed the likelihood of Brexit or simply missed the Trump presidential election. However, I digress...

For at their core, despite having vast regulatory competitive advantages delivered over generations of holding the governmental blob somewhat captive (in the "Stockholm syndrome" sense) the simple truth is that despite all their regulatory benefits, banks simply cannot compete in a modern electronic marketplace without changing their model wholesale.

Where the brilliant work in deregulating during the 1970's in the US and then the UK in the 1980's under Mrs Thatcher unleashed a whole new era of successful financial capitalist growth, the result was competitive markets that while propelling bank profits for some years post big bang, eventually it left the banks lagging, as their forte is process not innovation, inspiration or indeed anything which varies much from a very plain linear sailing path.

Banks have a clear opportunity to thrive and survive but they face a vast array of "Innovator's Dilemma" style problems...albeit without having much of the innovation ethos. Yes, yes, I know various banking C-suite folks in the later stages of heading towards pension approach and NEDs-ville are eager to have hipsters in a contemporary styled loft somewhere suitably edgy on the financial centre fringes with nifty espresso machines and a lot of pine in an effort to portray the bank being progressive but frankly we all know this is classic bank marketing lipgloss in almost every instance. The actual ethos for innovation, true genuine survival innovation is low. Apart from anything else that requires actual material change which is not popular by the time anybody hits the C-suite as they just want the comfy chair and to look down on the same old processes from their high altar of management oversight. Rather banks want to get as much lipstick on the pig as possible and hope to use their standard issue passive aggressive tendencies to bully or lobby their way out of trouble. Indeed their very regulatory status gives them a lot of power, particularly when faced by the abjectly incapable class of pygmies currently elected to high office in a tad too many major economies.

The bank which is actually super-innovative with a will to thrive – as opposed to the standard issue walrus with gaudy makeup and a desire to keep fighting for its place amongst the throng at the prom – has huge opportunity. Not as a big full service walrus – the era of bankosaurus rex is ending. Pick the right niches and banking licences will be great things. However as with all diet plans the best way to have a svelte fit frame is not to pack on several tonnes of carbs in the first place. Banks have been piling on the carbs for centuries and accelerating that process through mergers in particular for the past 50 years, with alacrity and monopolists' zeal. The difficulty therefore is all the legacy tosh which surrounds the banking system. Oh and actually the technology is only a fraction of that. That said, porcine lipstick aficionados will be quick to mouth a word like SWIFT for instance as a metaphor for everything lacking in banking technology. Actually for students of computing history (some might say digital archaeology), SWIFT have fascinating technology – with architectural origins in systems delivered by Burroughs in the early 1970's.

It is no surprise that the banking cycle has peaked because behind the swagger and bravado and the close contacts to government and central banks, the simple truth is banking is in a horrible mess. Fortunately propped up by an idiocracy masquerading as government in 2007, the system is rank, rotten, incompetent and fueled by abysmal technology on too many fronts including many of the systems around which the infrastructure of banking has been created. Oh and I still mean banking, I appreciate that sounded a lot like recent politics too. There are naive hipsters out there who seek to rebuild banking. Besides, it's a smart way to bet on the 'fintech' conference circuit as the people with the cash to splash on presentations et al are mostly banks looking for some more mascara to gloss over the cracks and (to put it mildly) blemishes. Or in the short term build something the banks think solves their problems and sell out – not such an ugly prospect to take the bankers' lucre methinks. However as a long-term solution, I doubt banks buying loss making unicorns with lots of promiscuous customers will prove to add much value long-term to anything...

Depressingly after 20 years of Capital Market Revolution! only a relative few financial practitioners are looking over the nearest horizon beyond justifying their mortgage payments towards actually seeing the future. The simple truth is banking has peaked and every discussion about finance from here on for the next few hundred years (egad!) can only be defined against the background of peak bank having been achieved just before the amazing self-inflicted wound of idiocy which was the 2007-2008 collapse.

Or, as Labour's then future PM Harold Wilson himself put it on October 1st 1963 at the British Labour Party conference:

"It is, of course, a cliche that we are living at a time of such rapid scientific change that our children are accepting as part of their everyday life things which would have been dismissed as science fiction a few years ago. We are living perhaps in a more rapid revolution than some of us realise. The period of 15 years from...1960 to the middle of the 1970s will embrace a period of technical change, particularly in industrial methods, greater than in the whole industrial revolution of the last 250 years. When you reckon, as it is calculated, that 97% of all scientists who have ever lived in the history of the world since the days of Euclid, Pythagoras and Archimedes, are alive and at work today, you get some idea of the rate of progress we have to face."[5]

Readers will recall that from the perspective of the late 2010's, the year 1975 when Harold Wilson was looking at the incredible era and pace of change, is nowadays regarded as an analogue backwater of stasis in technological terms. Few professions are remotely the same, albeit core banking could stake a fairly sound claim to have changed fundamentally little in the period since....

Besides, as already discussed the traditional bank was not a creation of the 1960's or the 1970's, it remains at its core a commercial enterprise fuelled by the accounting thoughts of Cotrugli, bound by the general principles of business established when the cutting

5. speech transcript http://nottspolitics.org/wp-content/uploads/2013/06/ Labours-Plan-for-science.pdf

edge of pharmaceutical medicine was a dose of leeches. The cycle has peaked – the bank is dead…or rather I suspect: long live the bank! In other words, there is going to be a big future for banks provided they can economically find their niche but the big plodding blob of all things to all folks is in exorable decline.

In essence, from the double entry book of accounting practice on it has been a bankers world. We have passed the peak of banking but Rome wasn't burnt in a day. Nowadays the power of digital technology leaves us in a situation where the mantra ought to be (with apologies to Dwight D. Eisenhower who has inspired my liberal use of his planning quotation):

"Banks are nothing, Banking is everything."

6. The Age of the Exchange

> "Do we need banks? Yes, or rather we
> need institutions to do what banks do."
>
> Harvard Business Review

Where Banks are nothing and banking is everything, it is vital to ensure that we do not lose sign of our relationship with money, investment and finance per se. Those aren't going away but they are undergoing a change as cataclysmic as the move from horsepower to the internal combustion engine and then some within the financial world. Thus, note how 1000 basis points is an exorbitant privilege beyond anything the digital world can handle. Having identified the peak of banking, please hang on to that bathwater full of historic business models… For the danger lurks that the 'baby' might be inadvertently tossed out too!

Attending any form of tech/startup/business conference in recent years it has been hard to avoid encountering a speaker whose vapid truisms amply demonstrate the legacy of linear thinking. Specifically this has been acutely true of the subject at hand. The story goes as follows: "Look at the model of modern business in the breathless startup tech age, hipsters, and, sheesh, it is just incredible, the largest of the unicorns include businesses like AirbBnB – an accommodation network which doesn't own any hotels! Or what about Uber, a taxi business which doesn't own a single taxi!" And thus the speaker hurtles into a series of further points which at once leave me wondering first whether modern education is worth a dime, or perhaps more aptly, a Satoshi. Second, I find myself reflecting on how poor the actual process of thinking is in the modern digital era. Maybe everything being computed digitally is not good for the brain. Food for thought.

Let's extrapolate this point about networks that don't own anything. I mean take that bastion of capitalism the New York Stock Exchange. It doesn't own a single share of the companies it lists or enables trading in. Gosh maybe that just proves... hold on... Certainly we seem to be on to something here. So let me see... AirBnB, Uber and the New York Stock Exchange just trade through as a form of agency the products which they specialise in. That product can be short stay accommodation, transit travel or indeed stocks and shares. Similarly eBay doesn't own the stuff it sells. Nor for that matter do Sothebys, Polish platform Allegro, MercadoLibre in Buenos Aires or China's Ali Baba and its sister company Ali Express. Titans of commerce one and all, yet without owning the stock in trade which they sell! There is a reason for this, a very very simple reason and it goes all the way back to the origins of commerce itself. The ancient Greeks called it the agora.

The agora sat at the epicentre of ancient Greek life in every city by the start of the classical period circa 600 B.C. It was where people came to read the new laws which were placed on display in full public view. The agora had fast food stalls akin to the modern mall. Rich and poor alike came to meet and chat, look for jobs and discuss scientific innovation or plain gossip. Generally the agora behaved like a social network, a jobs board and an epicentre for commerce. It was in essence an AirBnB, Uber and commodity market all rolled into one – and the agora itself didn't own a single room for rent nor for that matter a lectica or sedan chair to travel in (the ancient taxis even had crude odometers by the way, dropping stones from a hopper into a cup as the journey progressed).

In the often expansive confines of the agora there was a clear central marketplace for, well anything. They even sold some people which is rather frowned upon for understandable reasons today but the slave trade was active then. There was also an abundance of food and meat, commodities of all kinds including grain and textiles. In fact everything you needed to live including luxury products were present in a form of informal open outcry department store. While the agora was a fairly male dominated place, wealthy women often made trips to buy perfumes, silks and jewellery.

In essence, the agora was the forerunner of the exchange – the model of a fixed central location where trade could be conducted. The agora itself held no stock per se. It relied on merchants, slave owners and others to deliver the 'content.' I suppose we could then say it was very much like a mall where the shops are all tenanted. However there was an added vital social / business dimension. For the agora even played a role in the origination of venture capital and seed funding. Indeed investments and all kinds of transactions for tangible and intangible assets could be made in the agora. It was the bullion, stock, commodity and VC market with a healthy dose of lending opportunities to boot. In other words, the model for a centralised open outcry marketplace.

Returning to the present, the New York Stock Exchange is a hybrid for stock trading where the main building on Wall street stands as a beacon of free markets the world over. Like many exchanges the headquarters are now decorous landmarks with many staff but little actual trading within. NYSE retains a trading floor which is an elegant backdrop for digital news channels while the serious business is concentrated in the electronic marketplace. The actual electronic dealing takes place in the largest financial centre ever known to mankind.... and indeed the one financial centre nobody in finance has ever visited: Mahwah New Jersey, the epicentre of a vast data centre network which sucks up so many power there are concerns about electricity stability and sustainability in the tri State area if they keep expanding as rapidly as they have. Back to the floor beyond the bell ringing platform and the dramatic backdrop for television news, the overall exchange may be electronic for most business. However, the essence of the actual business conducted is remarkably similar to its origins in the agora...or even the earliest commodity markets which have been discerned between 4000 and

6000 years ago in Assyria, Babylonia, China, Egypt, Greece and Phoenicia, as well as along the Arabian peninsula. In essence multifaceted trade is the vital link which enables human life to enjoy civilisation beyond the natural habitat of the animal kingdom.

As civilisation has expanded, so too trade has grown exponentially in both scope and size, not to mention geography. Much of the trade growth in financial assets and obligations has been hand in hand with the money lending and banking system. Thus in the 1100s France had a system where courretiers de change managed portfolios of agricultural debts across the country on behalf of the banks. The courretiers could negotiate trades in these debts and thus became a form of proto-broker, in parallel with the Jewish moneylending benches which prevailed for similar transactions in the Italian city states. As early as the 13th century, merchants in Venice were trading government securities. Indeed, the history of governmental borrowing due to the monarch or state always needing more resources remains one of the few steady factors throughout the history of mercantile mankind. The trend for government debt trading soon reached the Italian cities of Florence, Genoa, Pisa and Verona amongst others.

With the age of exploration projecting the great leap forward in knowledge, research and of course commerce, exchanges reached their near contemporary form. Thus the hipsters of the 16th/17th century coffee shops became fascinated by the melding of modern financial products. Perhaps this was as much because the sludgy heated beverages they drank in said locales would be not remotely palatable to coffee enthusiasts today, whether drinking chain franchise Starbucks by the gallon or deep roasted Espressos by the dainty demi-tasse. In the square mile which represents the ancient City of London, the insurance market was born in Lloyds coffee house. When Edward Lloyd moved the cafe from its 1686 origins in Tower Street to Lombard Street in December 1691, a pulpit was installed from which maritime auction prices and shipping announcements would be made to the assembled throng.

Meanwhile nearby in Change Alley, Jonathan's Coffee shop had opened in 1680 and had a somewhat louche reputation – in 1696 several patrons were implicated in a plot to assassinate King William III. However in 1698, broker John Castaing took to posting the prices of stocks and commodities on lists inside Jonathan's every Tuesday and Friday. Soon some dealers expelled from the Royal Exchange for rowdiness migrated to Jonathan's while others went to Garraway's nearby. In 1773 when a group of brokers decided to erect their own building, it became briefly known as "New Jonathan's but was soon rebranded with a rather more imposing title "The Stock Exchange." Similar tales of the creation of bourses exist across the world and soon there were centres for trading stocks and bonds in hundreds of cities across the world. As discussed in "Capital Market Revolution!" the telegraph moved the exchanges into key centres – most acutely in the USA where the bulk of trading rapidly coalesced along the coasts. Commodity markets often remained close to the agriculture itself. Thus Chicago rapidly became the major centre in the USA for commodity trading, along with Minneapolis and Kansas, all being situated close to the lush grain fields of the mid west.

With the evolution of the telegraph, the bourse business made another great leap forward. At the same time, as noted in Capital Market Revolution! the actual exchanges themselves looked little different from the peak of the South Sea bubble in 1720 (or before) to the 1980s. Then whole new cathedrals of capitalism emerged as the derivatives revolution got under way in earnest with the likes of the London International Finance Futures Exchange ("LIFFE") being constructed in a form of integrated container inserted into the heart of Sir Thomas Gresham's commercial epicentre of the city of London, the Royal Exchange.

Yet the floor based practices looked remarkably similar to even a habitue of exchanges centuries earlier. Or, as the father of financial futures Dr Richard Sandor has been wont to note, if you read the classic Amsterdam floor tome "Confusion de Confusiones" from 1688, many of the central characters described could still be clearly recognised trading on the Chicago Board of Trade a mere 3 centuries later!

Apart from the Ferranti boards in place of chalked blackboards, and perhaps more nylon in the clothing, there was indeed little difference in the floor trader genus 1998 and his equivalent in the 19th, 18th or even 17th centuries. In essence exchanges had changed little. Yet their product reach was vastly different by the time the Capital Market Revolution was under way in the 1990's.

In CMR! I discussed the derivatives revolution but even then it was still often sneered at that somehow or other the process of predominantly men in brightly coloured jackets could somehow be driving a brave new world of finance. Yet this was precisely the case. This remains a derivatives world (perhaps now we are more acutely aware of it but not as much as might be expected a generation later) and indeed a world of opportunity – as per the mantras I chanted in the 1990s and still happily adhere to today. Indeed the floor based trading era, as can be seen clearly with the benefit of hindsight, 2020 vision if you like, while sensational to watch, was ultimately reaching their peak of processing during the late 1990s while chip processors adhered to Moore's law relentlessly doubling power and reducing cost to render human pit traders redundant. For one thing, the circuit boards and network cards didn't require much in the way of tea, coffee and lunch breaks while they weren't prone to social smoking or exchanging pleasantries in the local hosterlies either. Indeed the real quantum leap was the way electronic markets can deploy multiple functions simultaneously thus exponentially increasing market capacity. Whereas humans found it hard to function beyond a single pit, computers can effortlessly operate seamlessly across a vast, borderless, digital realm.

Here we arrive at what is a fascinating conundrum. For the original Capital Market Revolution! was undoubtedly critical of exchanges and sceptical of their ability to survive in the longer term. The general air of despair and the broad acquiescence of stasis apparent in many exchanges by the turn of the last century didn't augur well for bourses being big winners in the new century, let alone making much of a historical dent on a whole new millennium. Nevertheless, most of the big name exchanges have survived and thrived. True, most have substantially reformed but at the same time it is noticeable how relatively few of the new generation contenders emerged to challenge the old line monopolies.

In one sense this is broadly thanks to the incredible power of incumbency – and heavily regulated incumbency at that – AKA the same factor which elsewhere favours the banks. Nevertheless many exchanges created vast value in the move to for profit status which enriched many people, including a multiplicity of executives… it ought to be noted many of whom were frankly mystified why I was ever advocating the for profit exchange movement in the original Capital Market Revolution!

The early for profit exchange success OM was founded in 1984 by Olof Stenhammer in Stockholm. Earlier Stenhammer had become fascinated by options trading as one of the first registered brokers to the newly founded Chicago Board Options Exchange (CBOE). OM was the first for profit exchange to launch successfully as well as being an all electronic venture – albeit others had proposed such structures. As Stenhammer memorably notes: "We went all over the US and Europe to try to Find an execution and clearing system but we soon realized that we had to do our own thing." That "own thing" went live in 1985 as the OM Stockholm Exchange and spawned a myriad of installations in stock, bond, futures and options trading worldwide as OM, later OMX became the world's most broadly distributed benchmark of financial technology for exchanges and market structure, before OMX was acquired by NASDAQ in 2007.

The first electronic exchange to launch had been Intex, the year before OM on October 25th 1984 after a lengthy gestation of almost a decade. The Bermuda based exchange was founded by Junius "Jay" Peake who had made a submission about electronic trading to the CFTC in 1975 (Richard Sandor had first posited an electronic trading system for Californian commodities in 1970).

Nevertheless, the for profit model in exchanges remained a broadly alien concept to the 'clubs' which had prevailed for centuries and whose member systems allowed a close engagement to the system on behalf of the many individuals (particularly in the USA) who held the 'seats' (permits to trade) which were the lifeblood of accessing the floors.

As I outlined in the frontispieces, the 37th US president Richard Milhous Nixon unleashed a massive raft of deregulation of markets during his presidency. This action became critical for the development of markets and indeed the entire force of the Capital Market Revolution itself. The removal of the US from the gold standard by withdrawing from the Bretton Woods agreement has caused all manner of fiscal debate ever since. However its one clear action was to leave the US dollar as a free floating currency. Indeed, if anything, the free floating nature of the greenback only added to its lustre – at least in terms of global reach and usage – in subsequent years, as the US dollar has retained its dominance as a currency despite its demise being frequently predicted. In essence, other nations were forced to follow this fiat-based free market path and this provoked a whole new dynamism to the essence of borrowing and lending – the money market – itself. Of course a spin-off from the withdrawal from gold backed currency to a dash for fiat money has been a clear driver of the search for financial alternatives that has given us cryptocurrency – not just precious metal backed crypto either but other value systems such as Bitcoin, a restricted circulation coin based upon proof of work.

The move away from Bretton Woods was driven by the New Economic Policy where the "Nixon shock" was administered. In reality, Nixon was merely engineering the inevitable as the fixing of the US dollar to gold (at a congressionally-set price of $35 per ounce) was untenable. Much 1960s economic policy was devoted to dealing with a surplus of dollar supply which had resulted from foreign aid, cold war military spending and foreign investment. As a byproduct of the US attempts under Presidents John F Kennedy and Lyndon B Johnson to support the dollar and sustain Bretton Woods, laws restricting foreign lending and stemming the outflow of US dollars elegantly fuelled the offshore marketplace across the Atlantic centred around the UK. Thus the Eurodollar market was born and remained rooted to London where it helped the relative stasis of the post Imperial City of London find the first legs of a remarkable renaissance to become the world's most cosmopolitan financial centre by the mid-1980s.

From the perspective of the US Federal Reserve, by the late 1960's the US dollar was merely a bright lamp by a stream in summer, attracting not moths but vast quantities of opportunistic short sellers who were increasingly convinced the US government must devalue the dollar to match demand with its gold supply. The periodic runs on the dollar were a distraction from planning for the 1970's economy – what many at the time saw as the future 'white heat' of technology as Britain's Harold Wilson memorably opined.

Ultimately a run on the dollar provoked Nixon to convene a meeting of his top economic advisors in the heat of mid-summer, on August 13th 1971 at the Camp David Presidential retreat with the New Economic Plan being announced in a speech two days later called "The Challenge of Peace." At the core of the three pronged plan were tax cuts, a 90 day freeze on prices and wages. The latter was to be achieved via the suspension of the US dollar's convertibility into gold.

Thus the modern pure fiat money era was born. That said free floating currencies weren't quite there yet. Looking back it is intriguing to note how the world's elite at the time maintained a fixation with effectively fixing rates that nowadays we take for granted as they flow freely through the day from one 24 hour cycle to the next. A lengthy G10 debate resulted in a new list of fixed currency rates in December 1971 (and suspension of temporary US important tariffs in force since the August Camp David announcement) but by February 1973 this was already considerably revised as the US dollar came under further speculative pressure forcing devaluation. When this selling pressure failed to abate, the Bretton Woods process was a bare shell of its original aims. While some European nations tried to maintain a singular focus versus the US dollar in March 1973, the reality was, we had entered a new era of market-based free floating currency.

Perhaps the greatest irony of this system was that despite its inherent weakness as a currency at the time, the US dollar remained the world's reserve currency...even after it had abandoned being convertible to gold. What was a reserve currency pegged to gold remained so when essentially pegged to nothing more than the whim of the Federal Reserve Governors! Thus America's exorbitant privilege gave way to an even more remarkable version of the same thing, only this time without any tangible asset backing! Or I suppose one might argue the US managed to decentralize the gold backed system...but the end result was essentially the same with a forex market where the US was at the epicentre.

Speaking on television on Sunday, August 15, when American financial markets were closed, Nixon said the following:

"The third indispensable element in building the new prosperity is closely related to creating new jobs and halting inflation. We must protect the position of the American dollar as a pillar of monetary stability around the world.

In the past 7 years, there has been an average of one international monetary crisis every year... I have directed Secretary Connally to suspend temporarily the convertibility of the dollar into gold or other reserve assets, except in amounts and conditions determined to be in the interest of monetary stability and in the best interests of the United States.

Now, what is this action—which is very technical—what does it mean for you?

Let me lay to rest the bugaboo of what is called devaluation.

If you want to buy a foreign car or take a trip abroad, market conditions may cause your dollar to buy slightly less. But if you are among the overwhelming majority of Americans who buy

American-made products in America, your dollar will be worth just as much tomorrow as it is today.

The effect of this action, in other words, will be to stabilize the dollar."

In an echo of different times, the New York Times saluted the Republican President's bold actions at Camp David on August 15th, 1971 "We unhesitatingly applaud the boldness with which the President has moved" while the Dow Jones next day gained a then record one day uptick of 33 points.

This in, and of, itself may not have seemed overly seismic in terms of the impact it would have upon financial markets but the Nixonian revolution in financial structure was only at stage one. Forex fluctuations would now become a more real fact of life for exporters and importers across the world as merchants who had long grown used to relatively fixed currency values (albeit with occasional shocks in devaluation). However, having unleashed the power of the pure money conversion market, Nixon proceeded to reform the stock market ushering in what amounts to the birth of the modern market economy.

Under that elegant Buttonwood tree where the eponymous agreement was signed on May 17th 1792, the old guild protectionist instinct ran rife through the veins of the 24 proto-capitalists seated beneath the leafy boughs. The signatories agreed for instance not to undercut commissions below certain, rather generous levels. This era lasted for 183 years until the usually Communist-tinged festival, May 1st, was marked in 1975 in New York with shrieks of indignation from an apoplectic brokerage community whose regular oligopolistic stipends had been undermined by genuine free market capitalism!

Yes, I find it richly ironic too. At the cutting edge of markets until the 1970s, there was a de facto teamster union in pinstripe forcing commissions to be fixed at a rather lofty level. The death knell for fixed commissions had rung before, perhaps most notably when the Justice Department questioned the legality of such a process in 1968 and pressed the SEC to look into the anticompetitive nature of this institutionalised price fixing.

It had fallen to renegade NYSE President Robert Haack to be the visionary in the den of the linearly focussed. In a speech before the Economic Club of New York on November 17th 1970, he had noted:

"I am concerned lest we bask solely in the glory of the past, and in the process become oblivious to emerging trends. The New York Stock Exchange, to put it crassly, no longer has the only game in town."

However while many brokers retained the traditional "it won't happen here" attitude (qv attitudes to fintech in 1999), Merrill Lynch CEO Donald Regan, a future Treasury Secretary and White House Chief of Staff was listening where others were appalled. Rather Regan was appalled by the way the supposed capitalists of NYSE practised "cartelism" through fixed commission rates. Unlike others, Regan looked at the prospect of higher turnover through lower commissions. Haack / Regan's common sense approach to open markets was up against the seemingly immovable brokers whose cartel sought to hold the line like any good trade union picket.

Ultimately much of the brokerage industry was wrong footed by the removal of fixed commissions, convinced they would end up road kill as they struggled to make ends meet on reduced margins (fixed commissions were averaging one full percent remember) but while short term some retail traders even saw their brokerage fees tick up, the trend in fees was inexorably down even without any truly substantive addition of digital technology. When the latter started kicking in in earnest then we saw a further acceleration of fees, with costs to the client reducing from circa 80 cents 1975 to as little as 4 cents in the early years of the 21st century. In line with simple economics, where supply increases as costs decline, volumes soared and stockmarket participation exploded. Amongst the general public, whereas 15% of American households had exposure to equities in 1975, by 2005, that figure had risen to nearly 50%.

The Nixon deregulation created momentum for the Capital

Market Revolution! As the world of stock trading became unmasked it became clear that broking shares was in many respects a rather dull binary process, once the attraction of outsize commissions and the restrictions of the broker cartel were removed. At the same time, the sudden injection of a whole new realm of volatility in the world of foreign exchange was effectively like the opening of a waterway where previously the flow had been dammed. Here two effects were in force. For one, the deregulation of fixed commissions was generally accompanied by a removal of any quantity thresholds – i.e. exchange controls. (In Europe Mrs Thatcher pioneered this boon to trade within months of coming to power in the UK in 1979). The net effect of allowing money to flow on the path of least resistance between investment opportunities encouraged bankers and brokers to find ways to offer additional services to facilitate trade. Moreover as this nascent process of financial innovation took off it empowered intermediaries. Those with the most innovative products were able to charge the highest fees, thus making up in more complex transactions what was being lost in the plain vanilla of stockbroking.

Thus the Nixonian deregulatory era drove us to what I have long termed "a derivatives world." Over 20 years of Capital Market Revolution, the march of derivatives into the mainstream has been relentless. Yet, oxymoronically, they are still broadly reviled. Most often derivatives are given a hard time at European dinner parties where the guests are predominantly holders of fixed rate mortgages all delivering the modest miracle of interest rate rise mitigation, thanks to, well, derivatives... There is still some way to go before they have widespread respectability but as per my mantra I never ceased to proffer in 1999: this is a derivatives world. At the same time, educating more folk in society that money doesn't grow on trees and that government has not got a magic money tree to ensure prosperity, might be a good first step to helping expand the appreciation of how derivatives help stabilize costs for everything from air travel to weather dependent events.

While commodity derivatives had been in circulation in some shape or form since mankind looked ahead to the next harvest, the development of financial futures changed the exchange industry immeasurably. At first it was barely apparent. Indeed the legacy stock exchanges most displayed the sort of lack of foresight that would have wiped out entities with less incumbency cum regulatory protection to their mandate. The march towards a derivatives world created an explosion in new venues unseen for centuries.

Exchanges had been on a significant contraction over the twentieth century. Major financial centres became the epicentres of national stock exchanges and thus regional hubs in the UK (like Belfast and Edinburgh) dwindled as they did in Germany and many other nations. Bourses were quietly diminishing until we saw the emergence of the new derivatives era. Suddenly venues sprang up almost everywhere with member style models selling seats in everything from a venue in a Dublin cinema (never built – although as a child I recall watching "The Spy Who Loved Me" in the cinema during its heyday) to most every exotic island with a financial centre.

However, with hindsight it is clear that while the member model could be deployed, the real issue with new markets became access and scale – both of which required technology. Thus as the 1990's took hold the early internet demonstrated just how, at one, exchanges were hugely threatened and at the same time, presented a fascinating whiff of our digital future.

Indeed by the time "Capital Market Revolution!" was published July 1st, 1999, it was fascinating to see how the exchange world was broadly gripped by fear. True there were some optimists – the folks at EUREX were certainly convinced of their own survival – the Deutsche-Boerse likewise was being powered forward by its derivatives arm and its devotion to technology. Actually EUREX may have been more hubristic than merely considering their survival guaranteed but they had reason to see the power of technology having almost demolished London's financial futures marketplace. Nevertheless that London market, LIFFE was recovering fast and looking to the future with relish having endured that brush with near death which consumed much of the CMR! narrative itself. Over in the USA, in 1991, it may seem difficult to believe now but the Chicago Mercantile Exchange was close to a form of internecine civil war within the membership. Vast board splits had led to the election of a compromise candidate, brokerage boss Scott Gordon. While it is almost impossible nowadays to conceive of how the now 80 billion dollar leviathan CME Group could ever have been in such a situation, the reality is the exchange was challenged in direction and, rather akin to an aircraft carrier without destroyer support was felt to be almost adrift and at the mercy of the all conquering technological upstarts such as EUREX (who after all had only been in business since January 26th 1990, 120 years after the foundation of the Merc). Scott Gordon steadied the ship and set a clear course with CEO Jim McNulty. That revised CME prospers to this day.

In essence when Capital Market Revolution! was published it had a ready audience of anguished exchange bosses. Many saw the future, many didn't and indeed many still don't. Most worryingly not all of the latter group are retired. Nevertheless bosses like Luc Bertrand then at Montreal Exchange and Patrick Birley at SAFEX were making efforts to future proof their exchanges amongst others. However the number of generally forward looking exchange chiefs in 1999 was few and far between. On the clearing house front, perhaps the most forward looking was David Hardy whose offices at the London Clearing House were engaging the OTC markets with a view to clearing bilateral derivatives. Naturally, the OTC banks sought to protect their market position which was successful until the Pittsburgh G20 meeting marked the end of the previous 'hail Mary' approach to credit risk in the swaps and related markets following the collapse of Lehman Brothers in September 2008.

The issue for most CEOs at the time were clearly the threats in the ether – well actually for many exchanges, the threat was the ether. Full stop.

When assessing these threats at the time Capital Market

Revolution! was published – it is fair to say the results of the often breathless excitement of CMR! is now broadly in, a mere 20 years on. While absolutely buzzing with enthusiasm at the prospects for writing the book, it has to be said I wasn't sure too many incumbents would get their act together – hence the equally rather cynical side to that tome. Ultimately the largest 'casualties' mostly exited independent corporate life at hefty multiples… The arguments may rage on in many a conference – or perhaps after hours in the convention bar – for years to come as to just perhaps what the takeover prey could have amounted to had they but seen the light. That was the crying shame: vast avenues of economic potential were immolated on the altar of managements' broadly bereft of foresight and / or without the ability/motivation to take risks and progress their franchise. Take the case of the Chicago Board of Trade – the leading financial derivatives marketplace alongside the Chicago Mercantile Exchange for many years. Ultimately the end was a touch semi-ignominious for "the Board" as it was swallowed whole by "the Merc." – completing the deal only 7 years after CME itself had been on the verge of civil war due to its insecurity in the face of new technology. The richest irony is that having pointed out the CBOT would disappear if its management didn't get a grip, when proven right, many loyal Board-folk have yet to forgive me. Again, their loss. The same could be said of the London Stock Exchange, a kind of Spanish galleon of a behemoth in the 1990's which is now a credible standalone business thanks to precisely the actions it needed to resurrect itself and avoid being swallowed whole (as it has nearly been across several bids). Indeed the 1990s in exchanges now look like children's fairy tales to an adult – nobody seems to believe these conditions of confusion and entropy ever affected the bourse business….

In the end, national stock exchanges often survived the merger mania I prophesied in CMR! Indeed in the medium to long term the net results of cross border cash market mergers didn't overly sparkle in many cases. Rather regulatory fiat has often precluded vast cost rationalisation. In reality there appears to be a good argument that some businesses have become more focussed on costs and the bottom line without considering what might happen were their exchange subsidiaries to be truly given a growth mandate. At the same time, something I grew to appreciate over the past 20 years was just how truly vital the role of government remains in developing sound capital markets. Where government has played a keen role in making investment markets happen, great things can occur. Equally where government has been anti market, clearly capitalism doesn't flourish. Thus Poland before the round table helped deliver freedom, was as good an example of any from the Soviets of how the command economy delivers penury. After 1989 the government's commitment to the Warsaw Stock Exchange relaunched by Wieslaw Rozlucki serves as a magnificent example of just what markets can achieve. However the part which became clear to me in the past 20 years concerns the middle case. Where a government is ambivalent towards markets, then the markets themselves become semi-impotent. This is crystal clear in many of emerging European economies where government didn't grasp the Polish zeitgeist and embrace markets from the start. Likewise, even in advanced nations, it has been a frustration that the likes of Ireland has developed wondrous niche capital market services but the Irish Stock Exchange was almost never clearly recognised by the Dublin government for the worth it brings to the economy. In the end, the Irish SE slipped into the hands of an opportunistic bid from the continental federation powered by France, Euronext. I am not convinced this represents the best future opportunity for the Irish economy but it delivered a handy fillip to the Euronext balance sheet at a relatively low price. When it comes to government support for a market, the issue is not government subsidy or government money. Rather the issue is one of engagement. Sensibly ensuring the markets are aforethought in the government's mind, can deliver a great fillip in economic and investment engagement and thus returns for both investors and issuers alike...not forgetting the key benefits to the nation state itself. There is incidentally an amusing contradiction in terms here as the governmental regulations tend to favour incumbent exchanges hugely – particularly through traditional regulation – to deliver a national monopoly provider. Yet governments are all too frequently somewhat ambivalent about truly helping markets flourish...and then they restrict ownership of exchanges as if they are some precious national resource! Apathy tinged with hypocrisy or vice versa, the result is the same sluggish markets and a failure to exploit the ability to raise funding in debt and equity to power businesses to scale.

Given that many exchanges have been protected on the basis of the 'national airline' example only goes to show how vapid government thinking is towards markets in far too many cases. Having flown more than my share, particularly before the fierce competition of recent years, I have the air miles to show for my opinion! Thus SQ represents the great Singaporean city state in the air with national pride and perfection where the likes of the Luftwaffe remain a tawdry melange – good engineering, haphazard service and alas even occasionally dirty to the point of unsanitary, aeroplanes, all marked with a tinge of designer hostility towards the passengers (and I shudder to think what economy travel is like). A key remaining issue: for all the lip service many nations play to the concept of financial centres as a champion of some form, the simple truth is far far too many countries are neglecting their markets or lazily assuming that one bourse is enough no matter what its structure or approach to business. Meanwhile, the discount airlines have revolutionised markets and likewise discount players have changed the face of the traded markets including exchanges where they have been allowed to flourish without government intervention.

Thus looking back overall on how incumbent markets dealt with the threats of the revolution, I remain surprised just how many managed to survive. Of course many muddled through and continue to do so. However, as I have noted, mergers (as anticipated in CMR!) have become frequent throughout the 'parish' of bourses to the point where journalists are now barely unable to witness 2 exchange managers in casual conversation without believing a 'merger of equals' is afoot!

Yet the reality is the merger activity of bourses has ultimately become remarkably targeted – at least for the successful entities. There are some groups which have come (and gone) who acquired all manner of national assets but have often ended up with little more than a form of silo-hell. At the same time, various mutual era derivatives exchange managements from the 1990s retain a somewhat tarnished legacy for succumbing in many cases to the ghastly trend (which I always opposed) of cross-town mergers with cash market brethren. It was at least edifying on the various tours to promote Capital Market Revolution! To hear the audience mouthing along with one of my slogans from that time. Describing these short-termist and idiotic mergers I continue to believe "marrying your cousins does not necessarily improve the quality of the gene pool." Indeed on a simple point of history: it didn't. However it did allow a lot of remarkably 2 dimensional folks from cash markets to lead much larger exchange groups albeit often without much consequential understanding of what they were actually in charge of. This clearly has impacts upon how much growth can be realised. Indeed many exchange groups remain blighted by essentially two dimensional management when they need three dimensional derivatives thinking. However at the same time such is the robustness of the exchange model and its ability to scale that actually so long as you have a decent quantity of content, mix in some volatility and can distribute to a decent raft of intermediaries each with a broad client base... then you have a rollicking profit opportunity rolled up in regular incremental micropayments.

For now just park the point that as per the original CMR! and given my repetition of the "it's a derivatives world" message, the derivatization of the world remains a massive trend which has barely begun to reach its zenith even though it has already been playing out from the period when the Nixonian deregulatory measures were first witnessed in the foreign exchange and cash equity markets.

It is beyond the scope of this tome to delve overly deeply into the models of each and every exchange. However it is vital to understand that bourses are either like department stores or Anna Karenina, depending in which metaphor you find easiest to recall. Thus Anna Karenina syndrome based on the opening of Leo Tolstoy's magnificent novel "All happy families are alike; each unhappy family is unhappy in its own way." serves as a very simple understanding of exchanges. If you want to dig a little deeper, consider them as department stores. For no two department stores are quite the same, even though as British comedienne Victoria Wood famously noted "Whichever door you go in, it's always the leotard and handbag department."

In this remarkably globalised age of consumer products there is huge homogeneity to particular stores – a Nike outlet looks the same the world over (and seems to have the same hipster staff wherever you happen to be shopping). At the same time, each and every department store, is instantly recognisable as a department store while being entirely unique. Thus a visit to Galleries Lafayette in Paris is an entirely different experience to David Jones in Sydney or Harvey Nicholls and Harrods of London, let alone Fortuna & Mason in Piccadilly, Neiman Marcus in Chicago or Mitsukoshi in Tokyo. However allow somebody to stroll through any of them and they will immediately recognise that they belong to the department store genus.

The largest exchange groups are definitively department stores, carrying a broad line of products and services, but while there can be contiguous elements and firm overalps, no exchange group is exactly like the other groups. Thus the CME retains only derivatives and no cash while the likes of the Hong Kong exchange is a marvellous cornucopia of everything that you can imagine with a uniquely Hong Kong flavour (Neiman Marcus versus Lane Crawford if you will).

Equally Intercontinental Exchange is a fabulously exotic beast, exchanges across the world under the umbrella of a US multinational which actually has serious profit flows from its London and overseas offices. Amongst its portfolio of cash and particularly derivatives markets, clearing houses and so forth: its most powerful marque, the household name New York Stock Exchange is not the most profitable group business but a brand synonymous with stock trading the world over. The other clear stock market brand leader is of course London whose exchange group is again a vast cornucopia of interests but, due to a historical farago does not settle its own shares (unlike Deutsche Boerse for example). All these companies combine other interests – all do trading, some cash, some derivatives, some both, while some clear derivatives, some settle cash markets and others do neither. There are index creation interests and all manner of technology offshoots while the vast matter of moment is market data in a world increasingly focused on how computer power enables more data generation, leading to more data processing and thus delivers more data to analyze at every turn in the financial cycle often right down to every millisecond of the trading day.

So despite a uniformity of purpose as epicentres of investment and trading, exchanges have their own idiosyncrasies in all the major groups the world over. As we go down Young's Pyramid of exchanges, there is a variety of different operations and enterprises unified around the exchange.

I devised my eponymous pyramid as a tool to best illustrate the myriad of different entities in the exchange space. The difficulty was that public perceptions, particularly of brands, made it tricky to compare where the value really lay in investment terms and indeed the size of the markets themselves holistically.

I chose a simple basis – the value of the business (easy with publicly traded companies, a little less transparent with privately held entities). This is an easy metric to look across all the different units, particularly of the department stores.

The pyramid is pretty simple to understand but for added simplicity it has traditionally been broken into three sections. The entities in each section have changed rather a lot over time but the general principles have remained the same.

Young's Pyramid of Exchanges

Top Tier

Since the era of the 'for profit' publicly listed exchanges the lead group of exchanges quickly had 4 major members. That said the 4 bourses often changed...partly as value was discovered but most notably as mergers took place. Indeed it was only a few years back when we passed a fascinating point – the moment when merging two tier two exchanges would not automatically propel a unified bourse group into the leading group. At the time of writing, the top three has been very clearly defined for several years. The Chicago Mercantile Exchange powered by its colossal hold on derivatives trading, particularly in US dollars, leads the pack with the other two in the tier being Intercontinental Exchange and the Hong Kong Exchanges Group. All of these three entities are genuine department stores albeit with very significant differences to their make up. HKEX is a full house equity exchange plus derivatives with clearing house in that buzzing Chinese Special Administrative Region, whereas a lot of the balance sheet heft of CME and ICE emanates from their derivatives businesses. As this tome closed for press, the London Stock Exchange was attempting to vault into the lead group for the first time in publicly listed market history through a vast pivot into market data through acquiring Refinitiv, the Thomson Reuters financial group which has lurched from crisis to crisis for several decades but always proven as impossible to destroy as it has been to reform – subscription revenue remains a remarkable fillip to any balance sheet, even one which has been apparently losing market share since before I even began investing in financial markets as a schoolboy over 30 years ago.

Overall the biggest change during the for profit era, apart from various mergers has been the marked demise of Deutsche Boerse or DB1 as it is commonly known. When the Capital Market Revolution! was published DB1 looked to be unstoppably in the ascendant without any chance of being usurped. At that time there was more than a balance of probability that DB1 could become the predator that ate most other parties whole. Its trajectory towards world domination has, however, remained an ambition unfulfilled. Alas, in recent times, a decade or more of simply inert (at best) management allied with a lot of egotistically driven merger activity which was invariably unable to pass antitrust, has left DB1 now a pale shadow of its once seemingly inevitably omnipotent "A list" self.

Thus DB1 traditionally lurks at the top of the second ter of exchanges a little way ahead of the London Stock Exchange, some way adrift of the serious top tier players. Of course London's position may be that the LSEG propels itself up the pyramid firmly into the top tier on the back of Refinitiv's assets, albeit that will make the London Stock Exchange Group a unique department store in a different way with vastly more staff in the business of data than actually in the business of running markets or clearing services. Without Refinitiv, LSE and DB1 are good businesses but neither can qualify as a true A list entity. Likewise, NASDAQ, while a household name from recent times and a retail investor darling in much of the world, is a multi billion dollar business but a relatively modest property compared to the 3 major titans of CME, ICE and HKEX.

Second Tier

Within the second tier some 50 exchanges can be found. They are predominantly department stores, running all the way down to the relatively small but nonetheless significant entities of Athens and Warsaw – major market structures but within nations which are not currently major economies. In the middle of the second tier sits considerable emerging capital market potential, as evidenced by major markets in Brazil, India (several different entities) and Russia to name but three.

Third Tier

As we reach the third tier, the word "opportunity" screams out to me! Here we find around 500 different markets, from the world's emerging exchanges (such as Beirut, Buenos Aires, Sofia and Zagreb). The venues could be split by geography or product amongst other possibilities as the tier represents a cornucopia of wildly disparate venues, from the new swaps trading venues (SEFs) born in the wake of the immolation of various banks in 2008 through to specialist venues in particular product sets such as energy, electricity and emissions as well as established markets of smaller nations across Africa, post Communist eastern Europe et al Nowadays there are also a myriad of 'new new' things: exchanges built to trade cryptocurrencies for instance.

Indeed, at this point it is worth noting that despite the wave of merger mania which has grabbed many headlines for the past decade the most overlooked statistic is that there are more exchanges and similar market platforms in existence now 20 years after defining Capital Market Revolution! than ever before. Moreover that comes despite the heavy concentration of acquisitions at the upper end of the exchange marketplace for over a decade. The latter bald fact is often greeted with incredulity amongst market practitioners and therein we risk missing a key point in the digital marketplace narrative – the low cost of doing business in exchanges enables incredible possibilities for all manner of markets...

At which point it is worth returning to the original paragraphs of this chapter where I poured some scorn on the shallow conference speakers who have been staggered at AirBnB owning no hotel rooms nor Uber any cars etc. The simple takeaway is that AirBnB and Uber, let alone Mercado Libre in South America or Alibaba from China are all in their own ways exchanges or central platforms of some kind... In other words, the concept of the centralised marketplace is in vogue as never before whether as regulated entities such as the traditional stock, futures and options markets or way beyond regulated territory into hotel rooms, taxi cabs or all manner of consumer goods. Thus the conference concept of asset ownership at the basis of all business is a canard by those who haven't grasped a core facet of the revolution. This all the more remarkable given it was clear back in 1999 in "Capital Market Revolution!" that pure intermediaries had to add a lot of value to survive. Indeed at present in financial markets many intermediaries are exploiting their regulatory status or some form of market/ product monopoly/oligopoly, the latter prevalent with many commodity trading organisations. Whereas when it comes to finding what people want to trade: a simple honest intermediary looks like a broadly flat, open access, marketplace – a digital agora. Not everything has to follow an exchange model but then again many many aspects of investment powered by fintech are doing so in the revolution. Crowdfunding is just one of many many such examples. The exchange market works well as an epicentre where buyers and sellers can meet on an equal playing field, subject to a reasonable set of rules administered by officials whose aim is to foster more business. Therefore market operators appreciate they must engender ongoing trust to keep the marketplace thriving. An exchange has some reasonable elements of control over what product it trades and whether a crowdfunding project for the arts or shares in a new SME all the way through to listing a mega corporation on the NYSE, the precepts are the same. Moreover, the digital marketplace has one huge advantage: cost.

The greatest difficulty with exchanges since the agora has been the cost of their foundation. The barriers to entry for analogue markets included vast quantities of real estate and regulation has always been a relatively expensive factor. While the Greek agora had the benefit of often being largely open plan – and open to the elements – most countries have lacked the weather to support such trading: al fresco markets such as "the Curb Exchange" did exist on the corner of Broad Street and Exchange Place in Manhattan until 1921 when organisation ensued to place what became the American Stock Exchange firmly indoors . (hardly surprising given New York winter temperatures). Thus analogue exchanges required downtown office space that came at a premium rate and the technology they needed tended to be very expensive. Moreover, as exchanges specialised, they had specific areas for certain products all requiring significant manpower to broker and trade. That manpower was a considerable burden for both the exchange and the brokers and market makers required to populate every exchange floor. Nowadays electronic order routing can take the order direct from a customer anywhere in the world to execution while the market makers can be partially or fully automated, vastly reducing headcount for the provision of the liquidity lifeblood to make markets work.

Admittedly regulatory costs remain an ever increasing issue for regulated markets in the modern age. However, along with staff requirements, technology costs have come down enormously making it easier than ever to open new markets (I will spare you all the details but if you wish to build a new market, send me an email). Thus the only real difficulty in the exchange dating back to the agora and indeed pretty much ever since was its cost of creation.

Thus we sit in the age of the exchange. Even in the heart of the more radical thinking of cryptocurrency environs, there are those who seek to decentralize markets, for the core remains an "All2All" market model, albeit with distributed ownership and service provision across the entity itself. However this is the Age of the Exchange as the epicentre of global commerce across multiple channels. While the major markets may yet concentrate their assets further, antitrust issues appear to dog their steps with concentrated exchange acquisitions. In essence network power enables markets and that is driving down the cost of market creation. Moreover, digital markets allow unprecedented scale of access, whether to a granular or a global level.

The digital world thrives on trust, openness and efficiency. Nothing can deliver that better than an exchange whether it is AirBnB or NYSE.

That is why in every sense, this is the Age of the Exchange. Every intermediary more than ever before must justify their services between the client and the market…

"If history teaches anything, it is that central banks cannot take their powers for granted."

The Economist

7. Cryptocurrency - the Copernican Revolution in Finance

"At rest, however, in the middle of everything is the sun."

Nicolaus Copernicus

Doubtless there was a wave of excitement washing through the house on St Anna Street, in the magnificent walled city of Torun, a prosperous Hanseatic freshwater port on the Vistula river on February 19th, 1473. There Nicolaus Copernicus, welcomed his fourth child. His wife Barbara (nee Watzenrode) had given birth to a boy, joining a brother and 2 sisters. This youngest child would also be called Nicolaus. In due course, the legacy of Nicolaus junior would ultimately vastly eclipse his wealthy copper merchant father and all his siblings...albeit the extent of his achievements would not be clear for some decades after his death. However 500 years later his legacy looks to be securely on a trajectory towards eternal fame. For Copernicus lived the life of a remarkable polyglot and polymath. Nowadays we might term him the poster child of renaissance man perfection. After all, in essence his scientific discoveries helped propel the renaissance itself! Having studied at 4 universities across Poland and Italy, he had, however, relatively few formal qualifications – albeit Copernicus did achieve a doctorate in canon law. However in that era studying was seen as more important than the mere holding of a parchment of examined achievement. From his studies and judicious autodidacticism, Nicolaus Copernicus was an accomplished mathematician, astronomer, physician, classics scholar, translator, governor, diplomat, and economist.

Take economics for instance. In 1519 Copernicus developed a famous economic principle with origins dating back to classical times, in his treatise Monetae cudendae ratio ("On the Minting of Coin"). Copernicus expounded a theory later popularised as Gresham's Law by the Scottish economist Henry Dunning MacLeod (in memory of City of London titan Sir Thomas Gresham). In the same paper, Copernicus also formulated an early version of the quantity theory of money (the relation between the money supply, its velocity of circulation, price level and the output of the economy).

For most mere mortals this would be a sound basis for being in the historical record and maintained in most national dictionaries of biography for centuries. However it is essentially only another footnote in what was the truly prodigious career of Nicolaus Copernicus.

Copernicus' astronomical observations secured his greatest historical legacy. Most famously his final book: "De Revolutionibus Orbium Coelestium" ("On the Revolutions of the Heavenly Spheres") which was only published in the year of his death, went a long way to resolving the testy assertion by the Roman Catholic church that the earth was the epicentre of the universe around which everything moved. Rather Copernicus proved the theory of Heliocentricity. That said it really took the efforts of the German Johannes Kepler amongst a small group of other astronomers to popularize (and iron out some gremlins (beta errors one might say in modern tech jargon) of Copernican heliocentricity.

When Nicolaus Copernicus passed away on May 24th, 1543 following a stroke, there can be no doubt many mourned his considerable achievements. He had demonstrated a remarkable military command defeating the Teutonic knights in the Siege of Olsztyn between January and February 1521 for instance. However few, if any, of his mourners realised just how profound his contribution to the science of astronomy would ultimately prove.

Fast forward 473 years and I found myself at the most remarkable funeral mass. It was standing room only in the Gothic brick cathedral, the church of St John the Baptist and John the Evangelist which occupied a disproportionately vast block of land at the end of St Anna, or as it is now known, Copernicus Street. The church reached its current expanded form over 3 centuries on from the 13th century when it was founded as a small hall without aisles and with a polygonal presbytery. The great tower was completed during Copernicus' lifetime in 1500 AD with installation of the largest bell in Poland at the time. The Tuba Dei ("God's Trumpet") is a massive 7500 kilogram item cast in the city of Torun by local founder Martin Schmidt. This church indeed was where Nicolaus Copernicus was baptised (apparently in the 13th century baptismal font still preserved within the church). Now, on 19th February 2010, Nicolaus Copernicus had returned to Torun as a result of a remarkable journey of rehabilitation in the church following centuries of ostracism on account of his contentious heavenly theories. Bishop Reverend Andrzej Suski presided over a mass which was standing room only as well over a thousand people packed the church. Dignitaries from the medieval guilds of Torun lined up alongside the Bishopry, the military and judiciary. Indeed every walk of life where Copernicus had engaged was represented. Thus the remains of the great polyglot made a remarkable final journey which had encompassed much DNA testing to identify his remains and provide him with a burial place more befitting a great hero of renaissance science.

Months earlier, bones had been disinterred from under the floor of Frombork cathedral near the Baltic coast where Copernicus had been the church canon. While a standard procedure for canonical burial, after a near half millennium, the mood in the church towards Copernicus favoured a rapprochement from the era when his Copernican theory had been vilified by all parties from the Pope down in the decades after his death.

A marvellous coffin engraved with heliocentric motifs and carrying a facsimile of his portrait was carried from Torun by a cortege with military escort which took a lengthy tour around other key places from Copernicus' life. The journey ended back in

Frombork cathedral where Copernicus was reburied on Saturday May 22nd 2010. This time around, instead of being somewhat lackadaisically placed beneath the floor, Copernicus was given a black granite tombstone decorated with a model of the solar system commemorating his finest astronomical achievement. With the mass led by the Primate of Poland, Józef Kowalczyk, Copernicus' body was blessed with holy water in an elaborate ceremony where his rank as a church canon (removed in the midst of the heliocentricity hysteria at the Vatican) was also restored.

Jacek Jezierski, a local bishop who had encouraged the search for Copernicus' remains and his reinterment noted: "Today's funeral has symbolic value…Science and faith can be reconciled."

Indeed it was thanks to science that Copernicus' body was identified. Having been disinterred in 2005 after a year of searching, the bones of a 70 year old man were tested for DNA which matched hairs found in one of the books from his personal library, leading scientists to conclude that they had found Copernicus.

While working on theories which others had also been postulating, Nicolaus Copernicus neatly and elegantly upended conventional scientific understanding and repositioned the world in an entirely different universal scenario. It was a remarkable achievement even if Kepler had to tidy up some slight anomalies in planetary movement as he refined Copernicus' otherwise broadly accurate theory.

Clearly the Roman Catholic church didn't like the notion of their core teachings of geocentricity. At the same time, as Owen Gingerich noted in his excellent "The Book That Nobody Read" devoted to the separate lives of the first editions of Copernicus' magnum opus "De Revolutionibus," the church couldn't actually ignore the book entirely as the tables denoting the movements of the planets were in fact the best means to calculate appropriate festivals in the church calendar. Thus before the church relented and appreciated the heliocentric universe, they had a genuine "Catch 22" situation about "De Revolutionibus Orbium Coelestium."

While Copernicus delved into economic theory with some rather impressive results, at the same time, his impact on matters astronomical was clearly vast. In one fell swoop he successfully moved understanding about the universe from the flawed somewhat human-centric notion that planet Earth was at the centre of the universe, to an understanding that rather the Earth was just one of many planets orbiting the sun.

Or as Jon Stewart described it in The Daily Show:

"For most of our history we had grave misconceptions about exactly where Earth stood within the cosmos. Due to scientific limitations and more than a touch of narcissism, we believed everything in the universe literally revolved around us. It was a theory called geocentrism, which was originally egocentrism, but they spelled it wrong."

Egocentrism could be an appropriate word for a lot of human behaviour. Certainly within political scenarios it appears the ego of the great leader theory remains very valid and indeed the best politicians who achieve the most are all in their own ways remarkably charismatic figures who are not exactly bereft of an ego.

Given the trappings of office and the way the world's media falls over their every word – according it vast importance no matter what might be said – it would be hard not to develop a refined ego as a leading central banker in the modern age. True some may view the rather crass outpourings of fear masquerading as sapient analysis from the likes of outgoing Bank of England Governor Mark Carney (on everything from hysterical protestations of unproven economic meltdown at a UK Brexit referendum vote through to tree hugging hippy hogwash on the green economy far from his remit) as being a sign the central banker caste of recent times have overstepped the boundary of their influence.

Yet for all the vast deference accorded to the modern central bank Governor cadre, their profession is a remarkably new one. When Copernicus died in 1543, the bank had been long since established. With ancient Babylonian origins amongst moneylenders circa 1800

BC, if not before, there wasn't a lot new to banking which had seen its own early flowering of the Renaissance in Italy, particularly Florence, Genoa and Venice in the 12 and 13th centuries. Nevertheless Central banking was an unknown concept.

The generally accepted prototype central bank was established in 1609 – the Bank of Amsterdam was located in the Old Town Hall during a period of dizzy financial innovation as the Dutch empire expanded, only to be cut short by the peak of Tulipmania in February 1637. However the "Amsterdam Wisselbank" performed a series of functions of central banking which led in turn to the foundation of banks elsewhere in Europe such as the Sveriges Riksbank in Sweden (1668) and the Bank of England (1694). That said many of these banks lacked some core aspects of what would now be deemed central banking – the Sveriges Riksbank founded by Dutch-Latvian Johan Palmstruch lacked a monopoly over issuing bank notes until 1904 for instance. (Albeit a pedant would note the Bank of England is not a supreme monopolist of bank note issuance throughout Great Britain but has a regulatory control over commercial issuing banks in Scotland and Northern Ireland).

Thus the Bank of England became ostensibly the model upon which most central banks have been based. The Bank was devised by the 1st Earl of Halifax, Charles Montagu following a proposal by the banker William Paterson three years before which had not been pursued.

With public funds under duress and William III's government suffering what would amount to a 'junk' rating in the modern age, the British monarchy could not secure the 1.2 million pounds (very roughly 300,000,000 in today's money) it required to finance the ongoing nine years war against (who else?) the French. Montagu came up with the notion of proposing that the subscribers to the loan would be incorporated as "The Governor and Company of the Bank of England with long-term banking privileges including the issue of notes.

Those lending to the government would hand over bullion and

they would also issue notes against the government bonds which could be lent again. With the alacrity of modern day crowdfunding, a campaign grasped the public imagination through the equivalent of 17th century social media. Thus the required 1.2 million (300 million in modern money, remember) was raised in 12 days, with half going to the Royal Navy. Of the 1268 people who subscribed to ownership of the bank, 8 purchased the maximum permissible stake of 10,000 pounds (2.5 million in contemporary terms), including King William III, Queen Mary and Lord Commissioner of the Admiralty Alderman Sir John Houblon who would go on to become the first Governor from 1694-1697 as well as Lord Mayor of the City of London in 1695.

Nevertheless the Bank of England still did not have the functions of a modern central bank as a steward of the value of the national currency, nor as I noted above was it the sole authorised distributor of banknotes nor indeed was it the "lender of last resort." Thus modern central banking only evolved slowly through the 18th and 19th centuries. At the dawn of the 19th century, the once private institution which had had offices on Threadneedle Street since 1734 was viewed as a public authority imbued with the civic responsibility of maintaining a healthy financial system.

Meanwhile the development of central banks were helped along by a Copernican theme – merchant banker and monetary theorist Henry Thornton (described as the "Father of the modern central bank") touched on issues pertaining to Quantity Theory which was later more coherently tackled by the Swede Knut Wicksell. Thornton's 1802 work "An Enquiry into the Nature and Effects of the Paper Credit of Great Britain" wasn't quite "De Revolutionibus" but certainly he outlined the operations of the British monetary system and methods for the Bank of England to counteract fluctuations in the value of the Pound.

However modern central banking truly only got under way when the Bank Charter Act of 1844 was passed. This restricted banknote issuance in England and Wales to the Bank of England with a 100%

gold backing or allowing no more than 14 million pounds in government debt (circa £17,660,449,438.20 today – if only this provision had been allowed to remain in place! Rather the UK owes about 1.78 trillion – a solid three digits more than this limit!). The role of lender of last resort would only emerge after criticism of the banks' inadequate response to the Overend-Gurney collapse in 1866. Amidst criticism from amongst others, the journalist Walter Bagehot, the Bank adopted what has been described as Bagehot's dictum, described by Bank Deputy Governor Paul Tucker in 2009 as:

"[T]o avert panic, central banks should lend early and freely (ie without limit), to solvent firms, against good collateral, and at 'high rates.'

While central banks such as the Banque de France (1800) were also created as glorified war financing units, in essence 'modern' central banks didn't really start being founded until the nation states themselves attained their late 19th century border. Thus the National Bank of Serbia was founded in 1884 just a year before the first motorcar was completed by Karl Benz. The NBS was modelled on the National Bank of Belgium which itself had come into being in 1850. Those famed denizens of 20th century banking, the Swiss, only created their central bank over the winter of 1906-1907, mere months before the Paris-Peking motor rally became the talk of the tabloids as an adventure in extreme driving. Meanwhile the 500 lb gorilla of modern central banking, the Federal Reserve of the United States of America only came into being in 1913, on the eve of the First World War. Likewise Australia only created their Reserve Bank in 1920 and Canada, India and New Zealand launched their central banks in the wake of the Great Depression in 1934.

Central banking may infer it has been around for a long time but is a relatively young element of the financial firmament. Comparatively, bourses have been around much longer. The London Stock Exchange dates back to 1571, the Amsterdam Stock Exchange to 1602 and even the new world's 'arriviste' bourse, the New York Stock Exchange has its origins in the Buttonwood Agreement of

1792. Bourses are thus much older than central banks and indeed one might add, they have even earlier origins – Antwerp had an organised exchange in 1460 for instance. Commodity style exchanges within the bazaars of the orient and the ancient trading squares of Rome, Greece and Phoenicia as well as Egypt have been around for thousands of years...

More notably exchanges still have a long way to go. When it comes to the longevity of central banks, things are not so clear. At the very least their short term hubristic excesses of recent decades look likely victims of an impending recession, meltdown or worse. At the outside it may be that the game is rather up for central banks in many respects. Certainly there is a clear threat that the world can de facto disintermediate them. While all manner of outright monetary obligations have helped governments kick the can down the road of government debt, it is unclear just how long the bankers can retain their position as almost wizard-like grand viziers of the financial system. Certainly, apart from the wide ranging dicta of Mark Carney many of which have already proven beyond his material skills set – or at least his job description as a central banker (as opposed to his self-imposed task of being a kind of wet figleaf of absolutist trendy liberalism in the face of a real world doing its thing far beyond the fiscal crenelation of the Bank of England's semi-fortified headquarters).

On the basics of central banking, even central bankers have been somewhat questioning, if not downright pessimistic in recent years. Bank of England Chief Economist Andy Haldane has noted "central bankers may need to accept that their good old days – of adjusting interest rates to boost employment or contain inflation – may be gone for good.[1]

Or as the chief global economist for Standard & Poor's Paul Sheard

---

1. https://www.reuters.com/article/us-global-centralbanks/from-heroes-to-bystanders-central-banks-growth-challenge-idUSKCN0RV3G020151001

has pithily noted: "Memo to the human race: you tried all this monetary policy stuff... and at the end of the day it did not succeed in getting you back where you need to be."

The ECB's then Vice President (June 2010 until May 2018) Vitor Constancio told Reuters in 2015 "There are excessive expectations about what central banks can do," which at least suggests some Central Bankers are worried about their perceived status as superior fiscal beings, even if the remark came tinged with a degree of victimhood hardly becoming of those who live such gilded existences.

For a dose of greater realism, the Reserve Bank of Australia at the same time was more pragmatic. Reserve Bank of Australia governor (2006 to 2016) Glenn Stevens noted of the Central bankers' growth conundrum:

"We are unavoidably and inexorably being led to the question: how do we get more growth? Reasonable people get this. They also know, intuitively, that the kind of growth we want won't be delivered just by central bank adjustments."

We reached a de facto impasse by 2015, if not before. The Central Bankers had seemingly run their course in terms of what their monetary tinkering could actually successfully do to help the economy grow. At the same time, we had a somewhat geocentric fiscal world view. The Ptolemaic vision of money in essence saw central bankers at the epicentre of a universe which revolved around them. Thus the every last angling of paperclips appeared to be open to discussion when the high priests of money were expounding on their latest interest rate decisions after the ECB's monthly meetings. Fiscal Kremlinologists found themselves on CNBC discussing the deployment of apostrophes and general punctuation from the minutes of Fed or Bank of England interest rate meetings when they were published on a regular schedule in arrears of the meetings themselves. A vast theatrical circus that had evolved around the Central Bankers' hubristic egocentrism was perhaps the clearest vestige of economic growth actually delivered during the period when Central Bank governors stepped out of the shadows becoming some form of rock stars of the basis point universe. Demigods of money, despite the fact their relentless tinkering and gobbledygook left the world with more debt, less growth and arguably could have been dissembled in the advertising slogan "If King Canute did money management...:" Or, as James Grant the editor of "Grant's Interest Rate Observer" pithily notes with regard to the US central bank: "The dual mandate of the Fed is arsonist and fireman."

So the geocentric universe of great power vested in central bankers has not failed outright to the point where anarchy has emerged but it has essentially stalled. Who knows anarchy may come soon – as an outlook for modern central banking, I think Phillander Chase's maxim "Cheer up the worst is yet to come" may yet prove apt. Pure breeding thoroughbred bankers appears to have hit a form of DNA wall. Yet ultimately the 20th century and the beginning of the new millennium was characterised by the power of central bankers, particularly after the vogue for independent poilcymaking away from government really gained hold, led by New Zealand then the UK and Japan (the US Fed having long been independent). As the Economist noted in 2017

"Twenty years ago next month, the British government gave the Bank of England the freedom to set interest rates. That decision was part of a trend that made central bankers the most powerful financial actors on the planet, not only setting rates but also buying trillions of dollars' worth of assets, targeting exchange rates and managing the economic cycle."[2]

Ultimately while they retained their swagger with the Davos set through the decade after 2008, it was clear to most that the central banking geocentrist approach had run out of steam. Moreover, being seen as the architects of a rather one-sided system

2. economist.com/briefing/2017/04/27/the-history-of-central-banks

epitomised by the "Greenspan Put" many began to consider the central banking system a rather rigged game. In other words, where the central bank seeks to manipulate stock prices (or asset values more broadly) by lowering interest rates when share prices take a tumble, it appeared that come what may, in various guises, conventional bankers' investment mistakes would be bailed out at the expense of the citizenry. The shambolic reaction to the banking crisis of 2008 (led by Gordon "I saved the world" Brown amongst others) allowing mass bailouts of the failed blenders cum swap traders only served to reinforce the message that the banking system was rigged against the people. The vast asset bubble that has emerged since then under the decade long Quantitative Easing manipulation of money has only further suggested a system biased towards bankers and capital delivering a fig leaf of consideration for the wellbeing of the citizenry.

This era of central banking has been curiously at odds with the digital revolution. For the enabling power of technology has left us with lessons of leapfrogging – emerging economies making great leaps forward by missing out interim legacy technologies. For those who have been early adopters of technology in business, geography has been far from an impediment to improving the corporate or familial outlook through innovative approaches. Yet the Victorian supertanker of central banking has rumbled on. Central bankers have firmly occupied the interventionist epicentre of this geocentric approach to money with all power coming from the manipulations at the centre.

Revolutions aren't in the habit of gently tapping incumbents on the shoulder and suggesting they step aside for a fresh approach. At the same time, incumbents are rarely noted for giving up their levers of power without a struggle.

Moreover, revolutions are often driven from far outside the (frequently narrow and somewhat metropolitan) perspective of the influential oligarchy. Thus Copernicus produced his spectacular thinking miles from the largest European cities of his time such as Constantinople, Paris, Naples or Venice.

The Central banker geocentric model having reached the end of its lifetime, the difficulty has long been appreciating what might come next. Whether we see a massive explosion of asset prices to the downside and a major recession may cause a massive rupture or the rebalancing may take longer as QE deflates and too much of the global economy remains quasi-stagnant. A new age low interest rate stagflation of sorts has for instance left the European Union with a lost decade and more of economic performance where the best years have been little more than anaemic. There are those who see a swerve away from fiat money – currency without any formal underpinning asset – back to perhaps a gold standard or similar commodity backing. However being entirely centralised under some form of governmental entity hardly seems to fit with these cynical times where most consumers are only too well aware of the limitations, themselves described by Coperncan – Gresham law of currency debasement. Indeed the problem is that the citizens have lost faith in their bankers. The relationship with commercial deposit takers nowadays extends more because of regulatory safeguards such as deposit insurance than it does with any form of actual faith that the bank is a decent steward of money. This feeling directly correlates into central banking where the rock star hubris of many in the genus is seen as chillingly aloof from the workforce who needs banks, mortgages and a stable growing economy.

Equally it is only fair to suggest that while many users enjoy a single currency – the Euro for instance has at least led to the ability to cross many borders on the European continent without cause to change currency whereas a drive through the Benelux was a bewildering series of Guilders and multiple Francs only 20 years ago. However on the macro, it is difficult to have much faith in the political currency which is the Euro project given its profoundly flawed monetary basis and the ongoing Germano-centric manipulations to its existence, at the expense of peripheral states.

However where a single currency can be convenient, the digital world adds a certain optionality and complexity to many solutions. The same factors apply to money as indeed I originally argued in "Capital Market Revolution!" At the same time, the digital simplicity of online exchange mechanisms means the costs of transferring from one asset (or currency to another) is inherently low compared to old fashioned analogue methods – the problem with multiple national currencies is not their utility per se but the incoherent pricing of the many intermediaries in an analogue note-centric economy which provides forex kiosks with an opportunity to range from efficient servants of foreign exchange all the way to commercial operators on the Dick Turpin model as I noted earlier.

Within Capital Market Revolution! I sketched out 20 years ago a new world order of multiple competing currencies with ostensibly frictionless switching costs in real time. The currencies themselves might be based on fiat money or any form of asset or related instrument, including precious metals and other currencies. However I had left out one key element – which at least proves my e-money views were ahead of the curve but I am not the elusive Satoshi Nakomoto! While I could see competing issuers of multiple forms of digital currency – I called them Electronic Trading Units, or ETUs – as being eminently plausible, at the same time, the secret sauce – the difference between incremental change and revolution was within some cunning database driven technology. This we refer to nowadays as the Distributed Ledger or often by the moniker Blockchain.

Blockchain underpins the distributed nature of currency. The blockchain revolution began with a paper "Bitcoin: A Peer-to-Peer Electronic Cash System" by the pseudonymous Satoshi Nakamoto as follows:

"Abstract. A purely peer-to-peer version of electronic cash would allow online payments to be sent directly from one party to another without going through a financial institution. Digital signatures provide part of the solution, but the main benefits are lost if a trusted third party is still required to prevent double-spending. We propose a solution to the double-spending problem using a peer-to-peer network. The network timestamps transactions by hashing them into an ongoing chain of hash-based proof-of-work, forming a record that cannot be changed without redoing the proof-of-work. The longest chain not only serves as proof of the sequence of events witnessed, but proof that it came from the largest pool of CPU power. As long as a majority of CPU power is controlled by nodes that are not cooperating to attack the network, they'll generate the longest chain and outpace attackers. The network itself requires minimal structure. Messages are broadcast on a best effort basis, and nodes can leave and rejoin the network at will, accepting the longest proof-of-work chain as proof of what happened while they were gone."

As Nakamoto went on to explain in an online form:

"The root problem with conventional currency is all the trust that's required to make it work. The central bank must be trusted not to debase the currency, but the history of fiat currencies is full of breaches of that trust. Banks must be trusted to hold our money and transfer it electronically, but they lend it out in waves of credit bubbles with barely a fraction in reserve. We have to trust them with our privacy, trust them not to let identity thieves drain our accounts."

What sets Bitcoin apart is that it gave birth to the cryptocurrency movement enabling a decentralised currency. In other words a single central bank, or a single committee within a central bank let alone a Governor of a central bank is no longer the power in the chain of this currency. At the same time, the promise of Bitcoin was not in its singularity but rather in the way it effectively resets the geometry of the marketplace for cash. This, as readers of "Capital Market Revolution!" will recall, also unleashes an interesting new dynamic which the economist Friedrich Von Hayek eagerly espoused: the creation of competitive currencies thus driving greater efficiency in money but at the same time delivering potentially vast choice in how consumers and institutions can deposit their stores of value (let alone how they borrow).

In essence Bitcoin delivers its very own Copernican revolution. The whole notion of cryptocurrency entirely upends the old analogue somewhat Ptolemaic thinking of central bankers as the epicentre of money. With currencies which can be on a distributed ledger, the whole process of currency issuance become upended.

Rather than trusting a central bank institution, or even the demigod figurehead overseeing a central bank, a cryptocurrency de facto hands power back to the people – a range of people, a broad swathe of humankind, all of whom are part of the network operating each cryptocurrency network.

Thus the power to compete against existing national 'monopoly' fiat currencies (and supranational inventions such as the Euro) is emboldened through the benefits of cryptocurrency. The Federal Reserve or the Bank of England, amongst others, can call upon the implicit call option they have via the backstop of the government's balance sheet. Then again the cryptocurrency networks can call upon the faith they ought to generate by backing their cryptocurrencies with real assets. That makes for a very interesting counterpoint to forcing citizens to have blind faith in a government system which has demonstrated a studied history in spendthrift activity and irrational aspirations towards budgetary management.

In many of the Reddit outpourings attributed to Satoshi Nakamoto, the Bitcoin creator hit this prescient note: "A lot of people automatically dismiss e-currency as a lost cause because of all the companies that failed since the 1990's. I hope it's obvious it was only the centrally controlled nature of those systems that doomed them. I think this is the first time we're trying a decentralized, non-trust-based system."

It has to be said I suspect part of the previous e-currency failure was as much due to the concepts simply coming too early for widespread adoption as opposed to their decentralisation per se but that is a side argument as clearly Bitcoin has hit the mainstream in a fashion no electronic money had previously...

While many Bitcoin acolytes, particularly in the first wave of adoption clearly believed in the idea of Bitcoin as the unique crypto currency, it was always clear to me the BTC innovation had the power to fuel all manner of competing currencies. Open freely competing digital currencies create all manner of interesting positions with regards to the future of just what is currency and how it works. Please note that all these points terrify the living daylights out of conventional bankers and their regulatory cousins.

Indeed, for all their contemporary claims of the utmost sophistication (some may prefer to infer 'sophistry') money issuance was really conceived as a fairly simple process to facilitate trade. Once upon a time, currency was backed by something – well certainly something more substantive than the frequently elastic word of the government. Bullion – gold, silver and 'sound' assets that can be easily traded were originally preferred.

From the 1970's we came to rely on the era of 'fiat' money when thanks to Richard Nixon (him again) we saw the removal of the US dollar from the gold standard followed swiftly by the demise of bullion backed cash. Thus every government became reliant on their own central bank to issue money and, whatever extent of independence the central bankers had (in truth, statute or mere establishment hype) an ability to maintain value in money where they were gifted a monopoly in each nation to do so.

At the point of national monopoly, while it is still fashionable to trumpet state champions, the simple truth is national monopolies rarely find themselves successful in the long-term but they serve as a useful tool for government manipulation thus pleasing the control freakery of a certain timbre of politician. However with the digital world, the entire nature of the game becomes entirely international, if not purely global. In this theatre of monetary activity, in a micropayment, relatively frictionless and relatively real-time transactional environment, suddenly the competition for currency is open because an app on your cellphone is your wallet and it is broadly agnostic as to how you carry your money... Indeed the app's pure function is not merely to store your value but enable consumers to hold a potential infinity of different currencies in the palm of your hand... Note the prototypes of this approach are already in widespread adoption in certain quarters. Not merely as cryptocurrency wallets but in apps such as AliPay or indeed Yu'ebao, which we discussed earlier.

In recent times we have lived through a period where the central banking establishment has essentially failed the people (a few have benefitted from asset bubbles but many have been left behind, in the case of those under the suzerainty of the ECB et al in Greece and so forth: brutally left behind). The limitations of a Ptolemaic geocentric/egocentric central banking system have become all too apparent to normal consumers and entrepreneurs alike while bankers cling to the ongoing hope they can keep riding the wave of central banks being essentially destined to deliver banks' solvency and thus leveraged profits. This is, to put it mildly, a millennial perversion of the 'lender of last resort' concept. Meanwhile the political classes have gone from ostensibly liberal in the west to multiple essential tenets of a nanny state interventionism where contrary to the law of King Canute – everything can be controlled including money.

The ongoing technology revolution of the digital age around us is reshaping vast swathes of society. Meanwhile the appearance of imperial nudity at the central banker cum government nexus of fiscal responsibility is gaining vast credence amongst money folks and the general public alike. Just as nature abhors a vacuum, the digital process of distributed ledger brings a whole new solution which moves the business of money on its axes... Where we have had a vacuum of prudent money supply, there appears to be an app (or several) that are going to deliver a new age of 'safe' money.

Wherever there is access to a free internet, citizens are

increasingly able to interact freely with new forms of money – and that money can represent any form of underlying asset.

To return to The Economist: "Such debate is almost as old as central banking itself. Over more than 300 years, the power of central banks has ebbed and flowed as governments have by turns enhanced and restricted their responsibilities in response to economic necessity and intellectual fashion. Governments have asked central banks to pursue several goals at once: stabilising currencies; fighting inflation; safeguarding the financial system; coordinating policy with other countries; and reviving economies.

These goals are complex and not always complementary; it makes sense to put experts in charge."

At the same time, when The Economist mentions "experts in charge" British Cabinet Minister Michael Gove hit the nail on the head during June 2016 when he noted "I think the people in this country have had enough of experts with organisations from acronyms saying that they know what is best and getting it consistently wrong."

The issue is that now cryptocurrency threatens a whole new vista, currency which through the distributed ledger network, in essence reflects "The Wisdom of Crowds," and not the precisely formulated views of an expert central banker caste. When you take this into account, the digital revolution at its core powers competition and thus a whole new way of looking at money. Now if we layer on top the intrinsically trust-building network of decentralisation which is within the DLT/ Blockchain consensus algorithms, it only makes things more interesting. Whichever way you look at it, therefore, the final analysis is pretty clear. Where Copernicus realized the limitations of cosmological calculation and appreciated the true galactic order of planetary relationship, so the cryptocurrency birth, fuelled by the distributed ledger, can be strongly viewed as the Copernican Revolution in cash.

"Those who know that the consensus of many centuries has sanctioned the conception that the earth remains at rest in the middle of the heavens as its center, would, I reflected, regard it as an insane pronouncement if I made the opposite assertion: that the earth moves."

Nicolaus Copernicus

8. A Copernican Afterword

"While originally his findings that the Earth revolves around the Sun had angered the Roman Catholic Church and labelled him a heretic, this time his body was blessed with holy water and put to rest in an elaborate ceremony in the cathedral. His ranking as a church canon has also been restored. The mass was led by the new Primate of Poland, Józef Kowalczyk."

> The Krakow Post (reporting on the Saturday 22nd 2010 reburial of Nicolaus Copernicus 467 years after his death)[1]

I appreciate that turning the universe handily inside out wasn't what you probably signed up for when approaching a tome which might help explain Bitcoin, Blockchain and FinTech but it's a necessary evil of endeavouring to ensure the narrative delivers interesting insights that allow you to illuminate the other folks clustering at the water cooler as the day goes by. It's also a lot easier to remember than the sort of painful mansplaining which goes by the notion of precise technical description. Thus we have already made something not altogether unlike a quantum leap in thinking in under 200 pages. 'A small steps for the eyes, a giant step for financial thinking' to paraphrase a famous moon landing...albeit not that we have yet reached the point of 'so humdrum they are broadly forgotten' moon landings like the later Apollo missions whose astronauts are usually ideal material for quiz night victories...if only I could remember their names.

1. http://www.krakowpost.com/2102/2010/05

The one name clearly being recollected here is of course Nicolaus Copernicus, that autodidactical renaissance polyglot who guided the church away from looking at its planetary revolutions the wrong way around and has, half a millennium after his death equally enabled us to consider just how cryptocurrency moves conventional monetary thinking into a totally different orbital plane.

Or to put this all in the sort of dry prose variant of wordsmithery, the distributed ledger enables a decentralisation of the issuance of money which means a currency becomes essentially immune to the manipulations of currency issuers (politicians or central bankers etc) apart from how it is precisely defined within the contract governing the DLT currency itself.

Moreover, note that the currency can be nowadays operated by a "smart contract." This is an automated routine of programming which permits the definition of all parameters clearly and without prejudice to any holder. In other words, contemporary cryptocurrency can be created in such a way that it is predefined and therefore closed to manipulation. The most widely adopted smart contract cryptocurrency Ethereum was devised by Vitalik Buterin in 2013 who believed there was a need for a better scripting engine for decentralized applications. One interesting side benefit of Ethereum is that it uses "Gas", an internal transaction pricing mechanism which helps allocate resources on the network and thus enables efficiency.

Returning to the core concept of a smart contract, this means a blockchain based currency can be predefined to:

1. Link it to some form of underlying value
2. prevent it being manipulated
3. Distribute the currency across a network which is decentralized and thus beyond the control of any one party or even a group of stakeholders.
4. Actually do anything: you can automate into the behaviour of the coin... (it doesn't even have to be legal*

*albeit in the event you do program a non compliant coin, don't be surprised if sooner or later somebody holds you accountable perhaps with membership of the order of the orange jumpsuit: this book actively discourages non compliant coins and is not inciting any form of regulatory transgression!).

Before immediately pausing to wonder at the magnificence of such automated marvels as smart contracts, it is vital to appreciate that humans have to program the smart contracts themselves. Thus, "smart contracts" are only as good as their designers. The process of coherently designing and coding new cryptocurrencies / tokens is onerous. It's also quite different to how conventional coding works. After all coding a decentralized app is, well, decentralized by its very nature. That alters the way it needs to be designed and created with optionality in the event of change. Thus standard binary coders can come horribly unstuck very rapidly, as I have seen first hand when coders less capable of lateral thought come into contact with Ethereum and think 'easy peasy' without considering the broad gamut of outcomes.

Smart contracts need to have all manner of optionality built in – including even potential kill switches in the event of Armageddon or indeed some corporate action… Many ERC-20 (the Ethereum blockchain) tokens have been produced with dumb errors and then the issuers have all manner of problems. I have witnessed at first hand overconfident fast talking programmers who didn't understand what they were doing and the net result was not pretty.

Smart contracts are wonderful things but there are all manner of risks which require up front assessment and consideration to avoid – as once the code is 'in the wild' it can be impossible to amend when the process distributes. Moreover, as I can readily attest from the 2018 bull market bubble, there are some total charlatans out there claiming to understand smart contracts while producing tokens which are abysmally structured and/or coded.

Moreover, it is not just the code, the rules may themselves be open to some form of manipulation, making it important to have a clear understanding of just what makes a steady smart contract cum application and / or cryptocurrency. Then from the consumer standpoint, one cryptocurrency may look – or at least sound – a lot like another but they can have vast differences in their actual product, even if it ostensibly appears to be precisely the same!

Take gold for example. It's an element, it doesn't change according to where in the world you find it, once you have refined it to the classic 'four nines' (99.99% standard) but at the same time all manner or differences (perceived or more tangible) can exist pertaining to cryptocurrency. In fact from one gold cryptocurrency to another there can be vast differences. Amongst the various examples of gold-backed tokens which are de facto gold cryptocurrencies being offered have ranged from:

- The gold still in the ground AKA a form of equity securitisation of a mine.
- The gold is with a particular vault or network of vaults
- The gold is with a particular retailer or producer
- The token is itself based upon some form of gold contract or derivatives

That is just four examples but it gives us some reasonable ability to examine the merits of each in turn.

Where the gold is still in the ground, clearly there is a huge amount of trust involved...unless you have x-ray vision which can glance across the horizon and discern the quantity of gold in, well, 'them thar hills." Realistically there are many ways to estimate what is inside a mountain. This hill may turn out to contain gold, or some other form of less precious contents (like soil). This type of "gold coin" relies on a lot of faith as the history of mining is littered with cases where something went wrong. For one thing the estimates proved plainly wrong. Generally the optimistic nature of pre-sale of mineral resource land involves a degree of expectation inflation. In other words, the mine tends to deliver less gold.

On occasion there may be a bit more but thanks to what I might call the law of investor optimism, once something has been subject to the distribution of an investment document… well let's just say the number of underestimates of gold production are relatively few in my experience. So the problem with a big mountain and optimistic geologists leaves us with a huge potential to have mud on our faces not just within the allegedly resource rich hill in question.

Then there is the time and price issue to drag the gold out of the mountain in the first place. That may itself unlock a cornucopia of costs ranging from basic equipment through staffing and required energy. Lest it be forgotten, this invariably involves a hefty quantity of permits, health & safety plus all manner of ecological regulation. In the age of the drone, it's tough to just drill and live in hope no matter how remote you might feel your location is from an outpost of 'civilisation.'

Even once the gold is out of the ground a whole new range of risks emerge, from auditing the ore on its way to refining, the refining process itself… throughout a myriad of theft and other risks emerge. Moreover, this leaves our coin holders with an issue e.g. how does insurance work for the gold at any point to mitigate risk? The cost factor here may impact the gold token itself…and therefore the gold cryptocurrency may only be correlated to the price of gold (in any case delivering a purely backed token with an underlying has a form of basis risk pertaining to the concomitant costs around dealing with all the issues of a physical underlying. The trick is of course to keep this within the spread of wholesale or at worst retail prices for the commodity! In any case the entire process of mining then transporting and refining a coin from the mountain via the mine to be transported to the end warehouse is fraught with risks for a token which brings us neatly to the vaults.

Where the gold underpinning the currency is in a vault or network of vaults, at least we have greater transparency and more ability to monitor and control the underlying elemental Gold that it has the fabled four 9's (99.99%) purity. There must be control of the vaults and they need to be subject to security which itself involves costs for heat, light, staffing and the ever present health / safety and regulatory factors. However the end result is that this level of storage is fairly safe and transparent, albeit the underlying issuers need to have some element of planning in place to deal with contingencies, lest for example political upheaval stops a particular mine from being accessed (or leads to its confiscation by a truly rapine government), or indeed if, say a vault becomes contaminated by, say, radiation from a nearby nuclear waste spillage or even due to an outbreak of some kind of communicable disease amongst humans or livestock. For those who can't imagine such an outcome, remember that various financial districts were impinged by the likes of SARS in the past 20 years which provoked lock down of various financial districts.

Where the gold bullion rests with a particular retailer or producer, that company becomes a significant counterpart risk. As I mentioned above mining scandals are not rare. Canadian Bre-X was perhaps the most spectacular of these during the past 25 years. (Bre-X claimed to have a magnificent deposit at Busang in the forbidding Kalimantan jungle in Borneo, Malaysia sending its price soaring. A penny stock, its shares soared to 286.50 Canadian dollars and a market capitalisation of over 4 billion US dollars. Alas the samples proved to be fraudulent and the company collapsed, the geologist at the centre of the fraud, "Michael de Guzman, a polygamous, polyglot Filipino" (Washington Post) had tumbled to his death by jumping from a helicopter into the Bornean jungle in 1997.

Given the resultant chaos in the aftermath of the Bre-X fraud being uncovered, shares fell by 80% in such a fierce sell-off that the Toronto exchange had to halt trading four times, as the Washington Post noted "an embarrassment for a bourse that has prided itself on its technical savvy."[2]

2. washingtonpost.com/archive/politics/1997/04/16/after-the-gold-rush-fraud

Therefore a single point of storage especially where administered by a single entity without clear auditing may subject a cryptocurrency to issues of trust, if not outright mismanagement. Moreover, a single point of failure is an issue at odds with the power of the distributed network itself. All these factors are vital in the creation and coding of a new cryptocurrency if it is to be deemed better than existing alternatives, including government issued fiat currencies. Thus a cryptocurrency ought to be designed to be closed to manipulation as much as possible.

Finally if we look at the idea of some kind of contiguous relationship to the underlying this clearly raises separate issues. Thus creating a 'gold' cryptocurrency which is backed by a third party contract (e.g. a derivative) is also fraught with risks. This cryptocurrency concept has a dependency on the solvency and regulatory status of not merely the exchanges(s) where the gold derivatives are traded but more importantly the person who holds the accounts related to the exchange holdings in trust for the decentralised cryptocurrency.

Designing a perfect asset-backed cryptocurrency is difficult precisely because so much of its design through realisation involves a three dimensional process of management thinking. However, it can be done in such a way as to mitigate risk, maintain trust and maintain the value of the cryptocurrency itself. Equally, of course there are also 'proof of work' cryptocurrencies like Bitcoin where the currency is earned as a result of doing computations which help 'mine' new currency blocks and thus maintain the security and operation of the likes of Bitcoin itself.

So, while there is scope to make a flawed cryptocurrency (and I have seen them writ – or rather coded – large on my own screen), at the same time there is an incredible opportunity to craft a genuinely 'new, new thing' that competes with the existing fiat currency universe along the lines Hayek previously postulated.

At this stage, what I have posited as the Copernican Revolution in

Finance is overlaid with a secondary strand of Copernican thinking, our old friend the Copernican-Gresham law.

As I mentioned before, the Scottish economist Henry Dunning Macleod, popularised the concept after noted Tudor era City of London financier Sir Thomas Gresham (1519–1579). Nicolaus Copernicus discussed the concept in the year of Gresham's birth in his treatise on money Monetae cudendae ratio. While nowadays known as the Gresham-Copernicus law by many, the theory has much earlier origins, having been expressed in the Aristophanes play "The Frogs." In the course of making a similar point about men in public life, the Chorus says:

"The freedom of the city has often appeared to us to be similarly circumstanced with regard to the good and honourable citizens, as to the old coin and the new gold. For neither do we employ these at all, which are not adulterated, but the most excellent, as it appears, of all coins, and alone correctly struck, and proved by ringing everywhere, both among the Greeks and the barbarians, but this vile copper coin, struck but yesterday and lately with the vilest stamp;"[3]

Meanwhile Nicole Oresme discussed the concept in his treatise on the origin, nature, law, and alterations of money (De origine, natura, jure et mutationibus monetarum), which is one of the earliest manuscripts devoted to the subject of economics. This tome made a clear case for parallel currencies with Oresme viewing it as inherently normal to have coins made of gold, silver and copper all freely circulating simultaneously alongside other tokens of value with the market free to decide on the relative value of each.

Oresme went on to deliver his formulation of Gresham's Law thus: ". . . such alterations and debasements diminish the amount of gold and silver in the realm, since these metals, despite any embargo, are carried abroad, where they command a higher value. For men try

3. translation from Bohn's Classical Library

to take their money to the places where they believe it to be worth most. And this reduces the material for money in the realm."

Here Oresme notes something particular about the world of currency, in particular the regulatory stranglehold of 'legal tender' where a central authority (King, Queen, Prince, President or Prime Minister and their agents such as central bankers) are allowed to manipulate the coin and thus drive out the good money when they devalue the currency. Otherwise in a free market, of course, the price would be set by the value of the coin per se not the ostentatious aspirations of value forcibly ascribed through creating a money monopoly. In other words, inferior currencies are only allowed to survive precisely because they are government mandated.

Thus, having seen the further codification of the Gresham-Copernicus law, their notion that "Bad Money Drives Out Good" has been clear to see for some millennia. However the centralisation of money under the auspices of governments and – relatively recently in historical terms – their central bankers, has left the citizenry with little choice when it comes to holding currency. Citizens have seen fiat money being consistently devalued. However, holding commodities such as gold for everyday transactions has proven impractical due to storage and transaction costs alone.

However in the new digital age, the ability to create a new cryptocurrency does not have to fall within the purview of the government-central bank nexus. Yet it is very very difficult to fully restrict citizens from buying said currency. Even in nations where the internet has been censored to reduce transactions in Bitcoin, the reality has been a porous system where many have found ways to acquire digital currency.

Therefore in the sense of the Copernican Revolution in Finance, the moniker for cryptocurrency has in fact two clear attributes. The first is the power of the network driving currency to a decentralised universe away from the government / central bank nexus. At the same time, the second strand reinforcing that this cryptocurrency is the Copernican Revolution in finance relates to the Gresham-Copernicus law itself (with thanks to Aristophanes and Oresme).

In an analogue government-controlled centralised currency network, there is indeed a restriction how we can fight against the ongoing debasement of money, leading to an ongoing loop where "Bad money drives out good money."

Therein is of course the core trust element of all finance – something which appears to be too hastily forgotten by some governments until the market has turned upon them and delivered a vicious judgement towards crisis and restructuring.

However, the loop is effectively disintermediated when the Copernican Revolution in finance kicks in. The key is that without a manipulative centralised controller, there is an opportunity in cryptocurrency to avoid the same centralised manipulation. Likewise, the wonder of cryptocurrency is we reach the Hayekian nirvana of multiple competing currencies all fighting to be the store of value in our wallets as well as an instrument for transactions. Thus operating in a competitive realm of multiple currencies is in fact delightfully decentralised and presuming proper coding and design, will be subject to market valuations. Moreover they ought not to, by itself, merely depreciate at the whim of the established rulers.

Not only is this the Copernican Revolution in finance but in the wake of the Gresham-Copernicus hypothesis, I will postulate my own theory in this post Copernican financial world:

"Smart Money Drives Out 'Fiat' Currency."

Or perhaps:

"Smart Cryptocurrency Drives Out 'Fiat' Currency."

9. Tin Lizzie Bitcoin

"Ford reasoned that if each worker remained in one assigned place and performed one specific task, they could build automobiles more quickly and efficiently. To test his theory, in August 1913, he dragged a chassis by rope and windlass across the floor of his Highland Park plant-and modern mass production was born. At peak efficiency, the old system had spit out a finished Model T in 12 and a half working hours. The new system cut that time by more than half. Ford refined and perfected the system, and within a year it took just 93 minutes to make a car."

Entrepreneur Magazine[1]

Having advocated the inevitability of digital transformation in finance for some years before "Capital Market Revolution!" was published in 1999, it is fair to say that some folks have proven reticent even to this day to accept the vision of a brave new world digital world. In certain cases their reluctance to accept what I foresaw about the future of finance has been acutely marked by a myopia driven by pure self-interest. Thus fund managers rebelled viciously over my suggesting the likely extinction of 500 basis point entry/exit loads in unit trusts. In reality they were collapsing within months of "CMR!" being published in 1999 – not on account of the book per se, I had only observed what was inevitable. Likewise I have heard a great many arguments for the retention of floor traders – none survived a straight line impact with financial reality in the major diversified markets. If pit traders – or any other intermediary – didn't have a unique function, they lost their jobs. However that didn't stop

1. https://www.entrepreneur.com/article/197524

the likes one exchange staffer forcing me off the floor of the New York Mercantile Exchange...when ironically I was looking at new pit-related trading technology!

In other cases, I felt I may be verging on the cusp of being physically scarred for my views, even when they were delivered diplomatically. Amusingly, one of the arenas where I hit the greatest reluctance to accept my projections was at an event billed as promoting the brave new world vanguard of money a few years back. Yes indeed, when discussing the emergence of cryptocurrency, I faced one of the angriest moments of reaction to my considered remarks. This took place at one of, if not *the* first of the major Bitcoin fora in Poland. Poland adopted Bitcoin with a fervour which led a great many nations. However, on this day some of the audience went from delight to being markedly unhappy with my surmise of the future, to put it mildly!

This conference at Nicolaus Copernicus University in Torun on April 19th, 2013, was the first occasion I espoused my theory that Cryptocurrency amounted to the Copernican Revolution in Finance – a genuine shift from a centralised banker-governmental nexus to a distributed currency network where a decentralised power delivered a whole new currency opportunity.

The core of the presentation was rather short. Indeed the heliocentric nature of Bitcoin was espoused in just four slides. First there was the classic Copernican representation of the universe with the sun at the epicentre. This would become the background to the following slides. Then Polish Central Bank boss Marek Belka was pictured in the middle of this universe, after which I suggested he was the epicentre of the Zloty-verse and vital to Poland's economic fortunes. However, he was not as powerful as (cue new slide) then Federal Reserve chairman Ben Bernanke who was now central to the illustration: the Sun King of Central Bankers as he then was, reigning supreme. Albeit, I noted, 'the times they are a changing...' And then came the, er, money shot, as Ben Bernanke's hirsute visage gave way to a terrifyingly alternative illustration, a symbol of things to come. This was the brave new world going forward, at which stage, hey presto, the same heliocentric background reappeared only this time with the logo of Bitcoin at the epicentre of the universe.

This clearly tickled the distributed G spot of all concerned. The audience was fascinated and delighted to see a foreigner so clearly allude to the future of money with this splendid Polish-centric metaphor. The audience all but whooped and hollered their approval for the transition in money from the geocentric to the Copernican universe with Bitcoin at its epicentre looking to a distributed cryptocurrency universe orbiting around it. In the middle of a packed lecture hall, a row of frontiersmen types looked up from their specially secured heavy duty metal cased 'survivalist' laptops. They beamed in a mix of pride and admiration before they went back to studying their mining stats and the Bitcoin price on the rudimentary markets of the time.

Then came the sudden audience reversal. This took a lot less than the then prevalent circa 480 seconds of a Bitcoin block / settlement cycle. Moving on from the new Copernican shape of the currency universe, I rapidly began discussing the Hayekian dimension to the future of currency and imagined the excitement of a world where dozens of different currencies would compete equally for share of wallet.

Big mistake.

Following a collective intake of breath, there was one of those long silences across a huge swathe of the room which was amplified by a certain air of profound discomfort if not outright contempt. The frontiersmen stared at me in a mixture of confusion cum downright pity at how this speaker could elucidate some things so precisely and yet ignore the obvious point of cryptocurrency Messiahdom: the one true coin existed, why improve on the perfection of Bitcoin? Like a rival faith advocate at a religious meeting, I had uttered the most ludicrous notion to the true believer. This was a genuine blasphemy of then prevailing cryptocurrency wisdom. Stating that there would be other cryptocurrencies was tantamount to inferring that Bitcoin could be anything but a perfect singular solution to the future of money. There was no need for another cryptocurrency as Bitcoin was in essence, perfection.

Fast forward even 18 months and of course this audience response looked ludicrous. A swelling tsunami of new coins had begun flooding into the marketplace, entirely in keeping with the Hayekian principle of supply and competition. While vitally important in developing the cryptocurrency world, Bitcoin is really only the vital pathfinder which brought the notion of e-money and specifically DLT cryptocurrency to public attention. To examine why the singularity of Bitcoin was inevitably doomed, it is necessary to step back in our narrative to the pre-history of cryptocurrency and its digital origins from the dotcom bubble at the end of the last century. This marked the point where the first coherent attempts at a non-governmental global currency emerged.

* * *

"The operation of the Beenz economy will be terminated at 12.01am Eastern Standard Time on August 26 2001. No Beenz earning or spending transaction will be honoured after that date [...] Thank you for participating in the Beenz economy."

Over the years I have presented in 100 or so countries around the world (broadcast, podcast and webcast to many more too). Throughout that time I have been adding to my repository of currency stories concerning e-money in one form or another. "Capital Market Revolution!" was published at a time when I can recall seeing the sides of busses from London to Sydney adorned by exhortations to use "Beenz." At its peak, Beenz had offices in 15 countries, and operated in Australia, China, France, Germany, Italy, Japan, Singapore, Sweden, the UK and USA.

A prototype e-currency, Beenz.com was launched in 1999 with what was then a giddy 86 million dollars in funding from Softbank, Apax Partners, Vivendi, Oracle and other big VC firms. Beenz was a new form of digital currency with multiple core functions. For one thing it was a reward that accrued from purchases with particular vendors. You could also earn Beenz through spending time on websites or completing tasks. All the Beenz you earned were redeemable through conventional spending similar to other reward concepts such as frequent flyer miles or Green Shield stamps etc. Thus Beenz rewards could then be used as currency in its own right to shop at any stores which accepted Beenz. Therefore just as Bitcoin is a proof of work cryptocurrency, so too was Beenz in some modes (albeit Bitcoin is decentralised and the proof of work is innate to creation of new currency unit creation). By other measures, Beenz was also a proof of shopping / spending coin too – aka a conventional reward scheme. While Beenz came from the UK, meanwhile Flooz operated a similar model having launched a year earlier in the USA raising around 35 million dollars in backing. At its core, partners paid in the region of 1 cent to issue Beenz and then earned half a cent back when the currency was redeemed.

The concept proved popular and had some high profile supporters. While the actress Whoopi Goldberg was a paid ambassador fronting Flooz which remained essentially US-centric, Beenz attracted direct investment from the CEO of Oracle Larry Ellison who noted "Beenz.com is clearly an innovator by developing a true global Internet currency."

By a twist of fate both Beenz and Flooz closed on the same day: August 26th, 2001 as the dotcom bubble burst. Beenz and Flooz ran out of money. Flooz also found itself embroiled in a scandal where credit card thieves had managed to purchase 300,000 dollars of Flooz using stolen cards. This was clearly not an ideal look when endeavouring to engender trust in 'a brave new world of money' play.

Ultimately the first public chapter in the history of modern electronic money ended brutally at the end of summer 2001

"The international, 24-hour churn of e-commerce cried out for a monetary system that transcended borders and time zones. So in early 1996, Jackson began programming a back-end system for a new electronic currency, practicing medicine by day, and coding by night. He hired a software engineer to create the user interface, and four months later launched E-Gold."[2]

While not blessed with the similarly significant advertising budgets of Beenz and Floodz, two other entities deserve mention in the pathfinders of electronic currency. Asset backed electronic money was most notably debuted by e-gold which piqued the interest (one might add, the terminal interest to commercial continuation) of the US authorities, leading to a precipitate demise. Ultimately in the wake of the laws created to identify terrorist funding and other criminal activity post September 11, e-gold became an early victim of the ongoing urgency to identify money laundering...

Similarly before e-gold a venture called Digicash had proven unable to scale despite the rather fascinating – and very libertarian friendly – creation of a network of electronic money thanks to the genius of its founder David Chaum who was the first to use cryptographic protocols to help anonymise financial transactions on his network. The Digicash business was begun in 1989 in the same year as Tim Berners-Lee debuted the World Wide Web from his office at the CERN laboratory. In essence, Digicash was so far ahead of any form of WWW usage scale, let alone the emergence of web based internet e-commerce that it simply never gained sufficient traction.

The reasons for the failures of these forerunners of Bitcoin varied. Both Beenz and Flooz ran out of cash but the realpolitik behind their cash collapse could be best described as a form of 'duct tape programming' – in this case the process of synthesising stuff from the parts bin of life to shape the future. In essence the credit card companies pioneered online merchanting and all of a sudden their

2. Bullion and Bandits: The Improbable Rise and Fall of E-Gold
   https://www.wired.com/2009/06/e-gold/

prevailing network power of card users simply annihilated the attempts by Beenz and Flooz to create their own networks from scratch. The likes of e-gold tended to fall foul of US regulations as previously mentioned. Some see e-gold founder Douglas Jackson as a somewhat naive visionary who had long theorised on the foibles of fiat currency and the resilience of precious metals:

"Many a paper currency has spun out of orbit in a calamitous trajectory. "There has never been an instance of gold or silver being discarded as worthless."

Digicash, arguably the most brilliant of the bunch in the first wave of electronic online money, was simply vastly ahead of its time to gain sufficient adoption to survive and thrive. Nevertheless, lines in the sand were drawn akin to the Misrah Ghar il-Kbir "cart ruts" albeit nowadays everybody has forgotten quite what caused the lines in Malta in the first place. The same could not be said of electronic money. For the birth of cryptocurrency had already taken place in 2008 before the 2009 final demise of e-gold. Where Beenz, Digicash, e-gold and Floodz failed, Bitcoin went on to achieve a public coherence – and a full decade of longevity while still broadening its appeal – that eluded its predecessors. However, this leaves many wondering just what that impact of Bitcoin is and what it means for the cryptocurrency economy. To analyse that let's go back to the early 20th century and look at the automobile industry, successful after 20 years of automotive production but not yet ubiquitous...

Where others wanted to build exclusive wheels for the well heeled, Henry Ford identified the opportunity of motorising the American people. He was so successful he went a long way to motorising the entire world before World War 2 broke out and that conflict paused the growth of his empire and much else besides. Ford's breakthrough machine was the Model T introduced on October 1st, 1908. It remained in production for a remarkable 19 years, ending on May 26, 1927. In total some 15 million Ford Model T's were produced. Assembly stretched across the world. In addition to a plethora of manufacture and assembly plants across the USA as well as

Walkerville, Canada, the "Tin Lizzie" as it was nicknamed crossed the Atlantic to be assembled in Trafford Park, Manchester, England. Elsewhere Ford Model T's were put together in Argentina, Australia, Belgium, Brazil, Denmark, France, Germany, Ireland, Japan, Mexico, Norway and Spain. Ford often exported kits for assembly to these and other locations making the Model T the world's first truly global automobile. By the end of World War 1, half of all the cars on American roads were Model T's. By 1924 when Model T production surpassed 10 million it was estimated that half the world's automobiles were Ford Model T's!

Ford somewhat perfected the mass production techniques originally used for the Curved Dash Oldsmobile of 1901. Not only did Ford manufacture his cars ever faster as the production line concept was developed relentlessly in a quest for perfect construction, Ford maintained a reputation for a reliable automobile at a suitably attractive price. In essence, the Ford Model T was a car which helped propel the automotive age forward, motorising the middle classes of America.

Actually the roads were in many ways the problem for the "Tin Lizzie." However, the car was built to be robust on less than smooth surfaces. The design incorporated narrow wooden artillery wheels ideal for driving in muddy ruts and steel welded spoke wheels were only available in 1926 and 1927 at the very tail end of the Model T's production run. In empowering the American worker to have an automobile, many think of the Ford legacy in terms of its pure manufacturing achievements. However in many respects the impact of the Model T was much more societal. As Time Magazine noted in their book "The 100 Most Influential People of All Time:"

"He didn't invent the auto-mobile, but Henry Ford pretty much invented the modern world, transforming transportation and bringing manufacturing and society along for the ride. As Lee Iacocca, who began his auto career at Ford in the 1940s, wrote in Time, "The boss was a genius. He was an eccentric. He was no prince in his social attitudes and his politics. But Henry Ford's impact in history is almost unbelievable." In 1905, when Ford's backers insisted that the best way to increase profits was to build a car for the rich, he argued that the workers who built the cars ought to be able to afford one themselves."[3]

In creating the low-priced mass produced Ford Model T, the potential of driving and automobile ownership was now within reach for many more Americans. This had huge impacts on the US economy. For one thing it helped progress the campaign for better roads. This process had begun with Albert Pope's petition on behalf of cyclists in 1892 signed by 150,000 citizens. Civil war veteran Pope happened to own the USA's leading bicycle brand "Columbia" which was either a conflict of interest or a clever marketing channel which would today be seen as a move of 'influencer' greatness on digital social media. Ford clearly helped accelerate the process with his designs and his desire for every citizen to be able to purchase his automobile and enjoy the benefits of automation. Thus rural voters lobbied for paved roads with the catchy slogan "Get the farmers out of the mud!"

Helping build a more user-friendly expanded road network was one key factor but this then led to the second social dimension to the Ford Model T revolution. This process somewhat mirrored that driven by the creation of metro rail services and tramways. Thus the likes of Coney Island in Brooklyn, New York on the Atlantic ocean saw over a million visitors thanks to the Coney Island railroad service delivering passengers easily from New York City in 1875 alone. Hotels and amusements continued to expand and the railways enabled easier access for all social classes.

Such growth was clearly more restricted to where rail or tram lines actually travelled. With the development of the Model T Ford, the process became more multidimensional. Where a fixed position

3. http://newsfeed.time.com/2012/07/25/the-20-most-influential-americans-of-all-time/slide/henry-ford/

at the end of a railroad line made sense to garner business from passengers of the iron road powered by the steam horse, the automobile gave greater flexibility to the direction of travel. Car owners now had the opportunity to enjoy their days of leisure to traverse any part of the country – the key limitation being the state of the road and how much distance of travel this allowed at a reasonable speed. At this point the impact of the Ford Model T was simply seismic on American society and its economy. The freedom to drive in every sense fuelled an amazing era of development outside of main metropolitan areas. At first there was a smattering of roadside commerce – a handy means for farmers to bypass the local markets and sell their produce from the roadside. However soon it became apparent that drivers might also pay for oranges to be squeezed and juice pressed. They might like a coffee or tea to accompany this which could be washed down with a piece of cake... Come to think of it, raw vegetables could be cooked on the spot to accompany other local products in meal form... Thus was born the roadside service area, with restaurants, cafes, service stations and garages. From there the bed and breakfast and the roadside hotel / motel industry was spawned launching a whole new dimension of travel where people could drive by day, snooze at night in convenient accommodation and then continue their journey the next day. The continent of America, or at least some relatively modest components, became driving havens for a new breed of tourists as well as entrepreneurs and salesmen. In 1924, for instance the first A&W fast food restaurant in Sacramento California pioneered curbside service with their "tray boys" and "tray girls" serving food to customers in cars. The first drive-in restaurant was Kirby's Pig Stand, which opened in Dallas, Texas, in 1921. Kirby's rapidly expanded across the country using catchy slogans such as "Quick Curb Service" and "America's Motor Lunch" to drive home their accessible advantage for motorists seeking sustenance just off the highway. The drive through restaurant was a later development – nine years after the first Kirby's – in 1930 but it was first applied to banking (deposits only) at the Grand National Bank of St. Louis, Missouri in 1930. Drive through restaurants only came into being in 1947 in Springfield, Missouri when Sheldon "Red" Chaney, opened Red's Giant Hamburg on the iconic Route 66. To help people understand the many possibilities they could enjoy on their journeys, whole ranges of maps, driving guides and review books were published spawning a whole new dynamic for travel media.

Meanwhile on their cars themselves, all manner of new products became available to enhance the basic Ford Model T. A raft of 'after market' producers emerged, making accessories and enhancements of all kinds to cater to motoring enthusiasts, with parts aimed at making cars faster, smoother, more reliable, go longer distances or simply add some form of customised aesthetic to the basic Ford design.

Thus the Model T Ford brought driving to the masses through mass production and delivered an incredible fillip to commerce. This mass produced automotive revolution reached all elements of society. As well as proving the platform for all manner of business activities through Model T vans, even fire engines and so forth, there was a vast gasoline induced "multiplier effect." The Model T allowed drivers to explore and traverse America in a way that had never before been possible. This drove an improved road network but also had the remarkable impact of delivering mobility which led to more cafes, bars, restaurants and when night fell, hotels. This delivered increased opportunities to shop for produce as well as exploring commercial opportunities throughout the United States. In other words the Ford Model T was not merely a motor car, it was all in one a singularly astounding catalyst for the development of infrastructure in the public sector and particularly that wondrous wealth generator fuelled by human ingenuity, the private sector.

At which stage the narrative may seem to have strayed a long way from the travails of Digicash, Beenz, Flooz and e-gold. However our narrative concerning digital currency developed somewhat contiguously albeit a century later to the story of the Model T Ford.

First stage cryptocurrencies were somewhat like, the curved Dash Oldsmobile (a mass production pioneer but never the volume success of the later Ford Model T as it was aimed at a higher income bracket).

Drawing a line – no matter how circuitous it may look, from the Model T to the modern world, we find a curious linkage to that pioneering cryptocurrency Bitcoin, itself a refinement of earlier e-money efforts in gold, Beenz et al. In essence Bitcoin has done something akin to the Tin Lizzie trajectory but with money. Where Beenz was a curiosity and e-gold a fascinating segue, Bitcoin genuinely caught hold of sufficient public imagination to encourage all manner of enterprising individuals to start working on means to build the underpinnings of the broader crypto economy. This is why Bitcoin – whatever its future trajectory – is so different and indeed so vital to the cryptocurrency narrative. Therefore, just as Cryptocurrency represents the Copernican Revolution in Finance altering the epicentre of money away from the state towards private interests, so Bitcoin is the Model T Ford of cryptocurrency.

Of course Bitcoin hasn't helped with the invention of drive-ins or motels but when it comes to virtual real estate, it has done something very similar. Within months of their demise, the likes of Beenz and Digi Cash left behind less trace of their existence than can now be found in the South American jungles pertaining to tribes who died out centuries ago. Bitcoin on the other hand, became a network with sufficient size that it drove cryptocurrency into the public conscious. Moreover, at its core, Bitcoin built a network of miners who have proven eager to expand. Those mining rigs have also been put to work on a vast number of other coins helping mine and drive the transactional power of their networks. Before Bitcoin created a new decentralised fiscal process, P2P networks were anathema to the notion of money. With Bitcoin, gradually the world came to interact on a Peer to Peer basis, thus strengthening the network (I am not trying to write a precise history of electronic money – but for the record there were pioneers in the crypto space such as Adam Back who developed Hash Cash, Nick Szabo with Bit Gold and Wei Dai's b-money – all met the same fate of failing to build a sufficient network for one reason or another (or several). Szabo's Bit Gold for instance was never actually implemented. As digital power promoted peer 2 peer networks for almost anything, Bitcoin was the first to create a cohesive community for cash creation and commercial transactions that gained a broad base around the world.

That strengthening network led people to want to use different services – a classic facet of network power is how the original network often spins into different scenarios as the pure strength of the network grows. Thus Amazon began selling books but is now a form of one stop shop enabling e-commerce from Amazon's own warehouses but increasingly a vast network of sellers across the globe. The first real-world transaction in Bitcoin was made on 22 May 2010, when Laszlo Hanyecz bought two pizzas in Jacksonville, Florida for 10,000 BTC. All manner of e-commerce activities have taken place thereafter from buying items in online games through to a wide variety of substances, many of them illegal. In other words, Bitcoin is behaving just like the US dollar in this regard. However the really vital issue is that all this trade spurred more infrastructure around cryptocurrency. Thus the Bitcoin wallet was at first something which held only Bitcoin and was as clunky as the starting procedure of a veteran motor car (vehicles built before January 1st 1905). The quest for wider adoption and greater customer friendly functionality begat a series of wallets which hold a variety of cryptocurrencies. Those concerned about Anti Money Laundering and Know Your Client regulations could deploy a product from the likes of Coinfirm or Coinsillium to analyse the history of the blockchain.

(Contrary to a lot of widely held opinions, the digital blockchain holds all history on all transactions. True, wallets are de facto anonymous so it may be tricky to pinpoint just which individual or corporate entity was behind a transaction. However a spot of sleuthing can quickly isolate those Bitcoin which have found themselves involved in the dodgiest deals. That might not locate or identify the individual in question by name or address but it does allow potential transactional counterparties or financial intermediaries to understand how you have traded cryptocurrency and thus discern whether you appear to be a shady dealer or an above board digital currency advocate by analysing how your wallet transacted with other Bitcoin addresses).

In addition to the frontline wallet for spending and keeping your Bitcoin 'hot' (i.e. on the network and ready to use), a range of services have evolved to secure your digital money. In this sense the old fashioned physical safe has an online equivalent in 'cold storage' services where you can safely park your cryptocurrency away from the pickpocketing of digital theft. Other elements of the evolving Bitcoin universe included payment providers offering merchant services and indeed pretty much every facet of what is required to make Bitcoin an increasingly plausible alternative to conventional fiat currency. Thus the simple result of the scaled growth of Bitcoin through the world's digital channels has enabled a universe of services and infrastructure around the broader acceptance of the Nakamoto principals.

Equally it has to be said even just over a decade into the Bitcoin experience, the currency itself is not looking quite the fashionable young thing it was even a few years ago. Just as the Model T Ford was somewhat obsolete even in the relatively utilitarian end of the automobile market by its end of production in 1927, so too now Bitcoin is facing competition from brighter young cryptocurrencies. The power of innovation in cryptocurrency is not so far removed from what happened nearly a century ago in automotive development. The battle for Bitcoin dominance is akin to the battle of the Detroit automakers who expanded from Ford's 4 to Chevrolet and GM's 6 cylinder engines. Ford would then fight back with his V8. As we look at cryptocurrency today, Bitcoin has issues with its volatility which might be better served with say a cryptocurrency based on a more tangible underlying than pure graphical computational power – such as gold, perhaps. Equally there are problems with the scale of the original Bitcoin network and the operations thereof (without being too technical – you can search "block size limit" on Google / Duck Duck Go. A series of forks have already been proposed / occurred to try to enlarge the BTC network's scale of processing power as otherwise the feasible volume of transactions is significantly less than that demanded by wider usage). In essence the Ford Model T had narrow wooden wheels all the better to deal with muddy rutted roads but not so effective for speed and comfort on proper sealed tarmac roads. Bitcoin was an inspired vision of future money from Satoshi Nakomoto and a committee of excellent minds. The Ford Model T was an inspired vision for the future of mass motoring from Henry Ford and his staff. As I type about 18 million Bitcoin have been minted across the globe which compares with the 15 million Ford Model T's assembled around the world. Put simply, anytime 15 million or more consumers have acquired something it unleashes a lot of opportunity to harness the wisdom of crowds as every consumer has some opinion on what might be improved. This helps advance design incrementally all the way to the quantum level.

In essence, whether we look at design, features or popularity, there is in my mind a clear correlation between the mass produced utilitarian Ford Model T and Bitcoin. Both were trailblazers, both created a mass market where none had existed before and equally both effectively created an ecosystem which had not previously existed in the same size or form, helping progress commerce and develop the economic backbone of the age. Indeed the ecosystem surrounding the original product swiftly spiralled into areas well beyond the sector in which the product had been introduced, with ramifications for all mankind. Moreover, neither were pure inventions. Henry Ford merely produced a better assembly line and made the car something everybody could own. Likewise Bitcoin didn't invent electronic money or even cryptocurrency but it was the first to become ubiquitous like the Model T and it was the first to spawn a lasting legacy network of services, use cases and additional products.

Afterword: There is one final thing to consider when it comes to the Bitcoin as Ford Model T. I often ask the question at conferences: 'Would participants prefer to drive their current modern runabout home or take the Ford Model T?' I don't mean to make it a 'hair shirt' experience so we can talk about one of the later, more 'sophisticated' Model T's with a self starter as opposed to a crank handle, even the metal wheeled variant of 1926-27 if you prefer. So long as it came off a Ford production line, would you prefer to drive that home in place of your modern 'wheels?' However, even when offered the delightful coupe bodywork, or perhaps something convertible for summer...there has yet to be a single taker amongst the conventional fintech community for the opportunity to take the Model T as a swap for a modern daily driver. The remarkable point here pertains to automotive DNA. The Ford Model T shares considerably more 'automotive-DNA' as it were than modern homo sapiens with our neanderthal forebears for instance. Indeed the automotive "DNA" of the Ford Model T is hugely correlated with pretty much every modern internal combustion-engined car on the road. The engine is in the front, the seats and layout are the same as per the modern car – heavens a Model T saloon even affords the driver a height not far off that of a modern SUV. Certainly the relationship is vastly more than the sub-handful of percent of DNA we share with our pre-human forebears.

However, the desire to drive a car which lacks the creature comforts of nearly a century of evolution is low to non existent for every day usage. In essence the lack of customer convenience and comfort let alone the reliability of vehicles made without the benefit of multi-billions miles of travelled evolution during the past 100 years and more render the Model T unattractive for modern usage. Model T's may not always generously share some fluid through the bulkhead but at the same time they may not be overly comfortable in many climates (cold or warm) for driver and passengers alike.

Besides the lack of modern creature comforts (the Ford Model T didn't even have a movable driver's seat), information flow is sparse. Forget the radio, satnav and so forth, the standard early Tin Lizzie model was delivered without a speedometer, rev counter, fuel gauge or oil pressure indications...never mind the cornucopia of lights which nowadays let you know everything including when a tyre is feeling a fraction below optimal inflation. Actually the original Model T Ford was limited to an Ammeter – measuring the current between the battery and the voltage regulator. Nowadays of course modern cars survive without an ammeter – perhaps no bad thing – as we have become accustomed to a near perfect circuit of electricity powering ignition lights, air conditioning unit, stereo speakers for radio / podcasts while charging our mobiles, windscreen wipers et al. Besides, given that the Model T ammeter has a tendency to leap all over the place during driving it is fair to say some of the snowflake classes might be triggered by this and other rather rugged requirements to actually drive a Model T. That said as something of an enthusiast for old vehicles, I can readily attest that actually a Ford Model T is a remarkably pleasant drive – major caveat! – for a utilitarian vehicle of that period.

However let's face it with a puny by modern standards 20 HP (15 KW) and a top speed of 35-45 miles per hour (max 72 km/h) depending on the year built. The Model T may share a vast overlap of automotive DNA with today's road cars but it is hardly a challenger to compete for performance, comfort or fuel efficiency, let alone reliability (despite being excellent in its day) with a simple utilitarian Ford such as the modern Fiesta, or, say, the Toyota Yaris.

Which brings me to the future of Bitcoin. Actually, the stranglehold of Bitcoin on cryptocurrency was already breaking down during 2018, when Bitcoin hovered for first dropped below 50% of all pure cryptocurrency value being traded. Over time, I firmly expect Bitcoin will decline in market share. The price of Bitcoin may well increase but the share of the market will ensure a long, probably steady, downward path as new and exotic currencies, as well as simply better designed variations on the original proof of work Bitcoin theme are released as enhanced and more customer friendly cryptocurrencies. Therefore, while it was the trailblazer which popularised the whole notion of cryptocurrency and built a unique ecosystem around it which can now be shared in whole or part by other cryptocurrencies, Bitcoin – like the Ford Model T it shares so many dynamics with – will eventually become a historic artefact working its way gradually to the fringes of contemporary cryptocurrency but retaining its position in history as the Ford Model T of the cryptocurrency revolution. Will that be reflected in its value? Well naturally as all numismatists know, there is always value in old coinage even if it has long since ceased to be used as a daily currency.

10. The New Double Entry Book Keeping

"Accountants do a lot of transaction processing, reconciliation and control, and that could change significantly if this technology gets adopted on a widespread basis. The cost savings that the banks are looking at are huge, and most of that saving is people who do the back office, so whether you view those as accountants or ledgers, there's a degree of challenge to those in the accounting profession who work in finance functions."

Hywel Ball, UK head of audit, EY

Chapter 5 made some rather breathless pace through the history of bookkeeping and accounting. Benedetto Cotrugli, Marino de Raphaeli and Luca Pacioli all made star appearances. At the time they were active in the 15th century it was an embryonic place for the evolution of what might be termed early modern business in the early modern age but the origins of companies vastly pre-date the explosion in commercial activity initiated by the great leap forward on the commercial ledger.

In the modern age while some sole traders survive unincorporated it is hard to imagine much business taking place without a corporate structure in some form. The origins of the word corporation derives from the Latin word "corpus" or body. Thus the original body corporate represented a group of people who were authorised to act as one unit. The Romans first incorporated cities and then extended it to some community organisations with a variety of functions which they called collegia. Meanwhile private enterprises were enabled – called publicani – to contract for the building of aqueducts, arms manufacture and even social functions like feeding the geese in the city of Rome itself. Publicani were often loose entities, shifting coalitions of contractors who would join together to bid on particular contracts. Gradually the firms evolved into investor powered companies and there is evidence that some received a "habere corpus" status enabling a grant of limited liability for the investors.

By the time the double entry book keeping was under way, a popular modus operandi for mercantile commerce was through guilds. Through the middle ages guilds were chartered primarily to enforce monopolies in either specific verticals or geographic regions. A chartering authority (often a monarch) would deliver the monopoly in exchange for ongoing fees. While guild members might compete for business between each other, it was impossible for others to enter the trade without being elected a member of the guild. Trading guilds emerged, often termed regulated companies and they became a prototype of the company structures we are used to today. However regulated companies usually focussed on geography and thus the most famous of their early ilk include the likes of the East India company – a famous moniker borne by remarkable undertakings from each of two major imperial powers of the 17th century, England and Holland, both of which intended to diminish Portugal's hold on the lucrative spice trade.

Members of a regulated company, like their publicani forbears would often form short-term cooperative partnerships. Voyages of commercially oriented discovery were often funded thus, with pooled capital and limited liability for investors. Equity was subscribed by members at first but additional capital could be raised from outsiders as required. Ultimately regulated companies that sponsored equity-financed voyages came to be known as joint-stock companies. Each journey was initially separately subscribed – in essence crowdfunded – but as this was proving impractical, capital began to be rolled over from one successful voyage to another, leading to the evolution of permanent investor capital within these embryonic joint stock companies. The 'members' who crewed the ships increasingly became employees and managers of the company separate from the investors. Later, often as the industrial revolution took hold in the 19th century, jurisdictions created incorporation by registration – companies were created by signing up with a central government body through various paperwork filings. This removed the former privileged tier of associations being granted state monopolies for the pursuit of specific functions.

The precise history of the corporation remains somewhat contentious. Clearly the modern system can draw a linear relationship to the geographic monopolies like the East India companies on either side of the English channel. Nonetheless research[1] makes a strong case that the earliest corporations in the modern sense were to be found in 14th century Toulouse in south western France amidst the thriving textile industry.

Interestingly the world's five oldest businesses still in existence are all to be found in Japan. Kongo Gumi is the oldest, a construction company based in Osaka, which was founded in 578 AD. The controlling family sold out in 2006 AD after a period of financial difficulty to become a subsidiary of Takamatsu. The company has nearly 1500 years experience building Buddhist temples. Amongst the other five are three hotels (2nd oldest: Nishiyama Onsen Keiunkan, the world's oldest hotel, founded in 705 AD, still managed by the same family after 1300 years making for a dynasty which has clearly never troubled their school's career advice service) . Meanwhile the Koman hotel 717 and Hoshi hotel of 718 demonstrate there was clearly life in commercial innkeeping more than a millennia before Hilton, Marriott or St Regis. The fifth oldest

1. The Origins of Corporations - The Mills of Toulouse in the Middle Ages by Germain Sicard; Translated by Matthew Landry; Edited by William N. Goetzmann; with an Introduction by David Le Bris, William N. Goetzmann, and Sébastien Pouget, Yale University Press 2015

continuously running business on earth is Genda Shigyo a ceremonial paper goods company, founded in 771 AD which managed an early change management process when it moved headquarters to the then new capital of Japan, Kyoto.

However those with a fascination for shareholder joint stock companies will often point to the Swedish Stora Kopparberg ("great copper mountain") which retains a record of a 12.5% share stake being issued to the Bishop of Västerås in 1288 AD. The company was granted a Royal charter by Sweden's King Magnus IV in 1347. Stora also deserves plaudits for its ability to reinvent itself. From delivering two thirds of the world's production of copper during the 17th century, by 1731 the company had moved from that metal in relative decline to the more economically important iron ore which by the 1860s proved significantly more profitable than even copper. Having incorporated in the modern shareholder style as an "AB" company in 1862, Stora diversified further from mining to pulp and paper, almost entirely divesting itself of steel mills and mining during the 1970's. The copper mine closed in 1992. Nowadays Stora is part of the larger still Stora Enso as a result of a 1998 merger.

The definition of the corporation, with its unique cooperative characteristics have clearly helped spur simply incredible amounts of economic growth and development. The invention of limited liability was a brilliant component in the process of driving the company and prosperity forward. This was aided enormously by the ability to better understand the management of risks, assets and liabilities codified neatly through the double entry book keeping approach.

Interestingly in the era when Benedetto Cotrugli, Marino de Raphaeli and Luca Pacioli were playing a key role in codifying the accounting of mercantilism, they all understood the need for extending credit. In that sense, by balancing assets and liabilities, the merchant could, in essence, surreptitiously, extend credit. This of course was a delicate situation. For at the time the charging of interest was illegal. However the church's impositions were skirted elegantly through means of adding commissions or insurance premia to debts in ways which loaded a higher gross cost without being a pure interest coupon on the debt itself. Interestingly Cotrugli was also clear on the treatment of nonperforming loans – a 50% write-off after a year with the entire debt written off after 24 months had elapsed: "because for the merchant losing time and losing money are the same thing."

Of course the initial double entry book keeping theory has since been enormously evolved but it remains in essence the same system as De Rafaeli et al. Some of the techniques deployed by De Rafaeli for important accounting projects at the time have fallen into disuse in the modern era. Take "Dowry Accounting" for instance – something which lost popularity in christian nations long before the "#metoo" era befell Hollywood producers and many joint stock companies across the world. Nowadays it would be hard to find somebody in much of the world who requires input on how much of a dowry ought to be repaid on the premature death of a bride. Likewise the tricky question of resolving the pass through payments for a widow who remarries were once a thorny issue but not so much today it seems. It is interesting to note – and a good sign of the lack of sophistication in the time before limited liability caught on in mercantile life – that merchants taught by pioneers like De Rafaeli did not separate their household accounting from their business accounts. Thus a major source of conflict of interest was apparent in the earliest accounts, one which continues to cause issues to this day.

Thus without the development of that central ledger to accompany the basic accounting balance sheet, it is difficult to see how any form of business, risk management and particularly financial activity could have feasibly evolved. Without the development of double entry book keeping it would have left the mathematics of commerce essentially in a limbo akin to those cultures with only an oral culture and no developed habit of writing.

Leaping a half millennia or more from the deep analogue to the early flowering of the digital world, the latest thinking in accounting has added a whole new layer to the double entry. If we take our new friend, the blockchain, double entry bookkeeping can become triple entry bookkeeping. A key facet to the blockchain is the immutable nature of the ledger. That the blockchain cannot be changed without leaving traces of amendment – and only amended by those permissioned to do so – is in and of itself highly useful. Moreover, the digital nature of a networked blockchain mean it is immediately accessible by a raft of participants / stakeholders in real time. This adds confidence and hugely reduces the opportunity to change the record whether for nefarious benefit or otherwise. Or to put it another way: Welcome to a third dimension in accounting.

History and perspective were clearly created in the original ledger which drove the double entry revolution. However this was centralised around the merchant reflecting his world view – a monopersective if you will. In other words, one merchant saw his accounts purely in his perceived reflection of self interest. Meanwhile, the merchant next door – perhaps even the merchant on the next bench in the market – might have a completely different view of the status of his accounts, even where it involved the neighbouring merchant. Going back to the Magic Post-it Note explanation of the blockchain itself I outlined earlier, it is worth remembering that the trust element of the DLT delivers a whole added standard of protection, as does the immutability factor to any blockchain data updates. Now this infuses accounting with a whole new realm of factors which fundamentally improve data, and indeed accounts.

Thus the third level of accounting via a blockchain ledger delivers an all new real time potential for accounting. Some might see it as akin to those "just in time" methodologies popularised by motor manufacturers like Toyota. In many ways this is more than merely 'just in time accounting' delivered across a global network (or as far as the company requires), A Blockchain tier can help deliver a better quality to accounting and particularly auditing just when the profession of auditing has been somewhat struggling in the reputation stakes after a series of high profile frauds this century beginning with Enron, Tyco and Worldcom amidst the dotcom bubble casualties on the cusp of the new millennium. At a point where the audit profession has never looked more exposed to ridicule, the delivery of a third tier blockchain auditing movement could be not merely a saviour for the broadly discredited audit profession, it could also be a great boost to investor and counterparty confidence.

Indeed, there are a variety of ways in which the blockchain might help accounting and auditing in the future. For one thing there is always the possibility of a massive singular blockchain which might record all parties' records of every transaction. That said, I am sceptical that there is ever much of a pure singularity of anything in the commercial world – apart from the fact that antitrust gets nervous once anybody holds 40% of any market...Thus a singular megachain looks implausible, unless Darth Vader manages to run the universe...and even there some say he would face a lot of problems with resistance forces across the years.

However, for auditors within a company – no matter how large and globally diverse that corporation may be – it is fair to believe companies may do all their internal accounts on a blockchain which relates all arms of a traditional multinational into essentially one system. That could provide huge amounts of data and be a massive boon for auditors, providing immutable evidence of transactions and their documentation. However, the auditing profession itself might not see such vast profits in the future for the simple reason that the delivery of all accounting into a DLT system would enable vast amounts of automated data processing to take place to check flows and related payments – in essence 'bots can disintermediate the human auditors who have only ever been able to 'sample' data within large and complex companies. Nevertheless, the opportunity is there for vastly improved audit procedures to root out fraud and mismanagement – quite feasibly before the traditional quarterly accounting or annual audit periods take place. In that sense the audit process will improve, the auditors will have to live with lower charges and more automation which will reduce the headcounts of audit firms and indeed lower corporate costs of compliance. This is – arguably, unless you are a junior auditor – a "win win."

Certainly the use of blockchain could vastly reduce the significant number of human errors on the input side from the corporate side. With the right application of DLT technology it ought to be easier to root out managers who are inflating reports compared to the underlying cash flow – as after all there would be a suitably formatted immutable stream of information from the company treasury and the banks. Ideally this is going to occur in something as close as possible to real time.

In a 2016 San Francisco TedX talk "Blockchain Revolution" author Don Tapscott jr noted "Accounting is basically broken…" Going on to note when it comes to "human error, 35% of accounting fraud is actually due to some unintentional mistake. Poor Pam in the back office fat fingers an entry into an Excel spreadsheet and like a butterfly flapping its wings it reverberates across the whole enterprise and creates a big crisis…. The big issue is that modern accounting practices can't really keep up with the velocity and the complexity of companies and businesses and deciphering a financial statement is kind of like watching two people dancing under a strobe light. You see bits and pieces, an arm, a head you know someone is shaking their booty but you don't actually get the whole picture because accounting is based on a principle that's actually quite ancient."

It would be unfair to heap scorn on the double entry bookkeeping method at this juncture. After all it has remained the epicentre of accounting essentially unchanged for 600 years because it is a sound basis for managing mercantile practices. It has proven itself sublimely robust in a world which its inventors could not have imagined 6 centuries ago. However the world has moved on in leaps and bounds…double entry is one of those few unique practices which was so good at inception that nobody has actually improved on it. In that respect double entry book keeping is the corporate equivalent of the legendary Stradivarius violins dating back to the 17th century – deemed to have an unparalleled sound quality compared even with modern instruments. The double entry method struck a numerical chord with commercial common sense which has given it considerable utility – and global ubiquity – ever since.

However with the blockchain suddenly data goes multidimensional and that provides a massive opportunity to improve accounting and auditing with a series of keystrokes. The debit and credit data remains but now it is time stamped for accuracy of input, with details of who entered the data, from which point on the network, based on what data… More significantly all that data is immutable. Yes of course a subsequent update can note when Eric in accounts mistyped a billion instead of a million but the error will be clearly recorded. Then there is transparency of the problem which arose and the solution which was deployed (and by whom – in this case presumably a supervisor). The trust in the ledger would be considerable and suddenly accounts could regain their position as being something which could be credibly audited, as opposed to the modern human interventions which amount to something not awfully different to delivering a set of principles and then sampling the cookie mix at judicious points on the production line to ensure it is a decent batch of credible cake headed to the oven. Indeed accounts themselves could start to morph to some degree away from the current out-of-date-by the time they are published quarterly, semi-annual or annual snapshots of the enterprise into a much more dynamic real time environment. However that's probably a little bit too close to the moon shot end of the spectrum at least for current public consumption. AKA I doubt we will start seeing monthly results calls. Quarterly is already more than enough in the current stock market world charged with regulation from the dotcom bubble's juvenile excesses at the turn of the century! The key thing to bear in mind is that where double entry book keeping introduced a ledger and became the explosive underpinning of the mercantile economy, ably supported by the principle of limited liability...now DLT takes the whole adventure into the digital age.

Thus Bitcoin forms the Model T Ford of cryptocurrency which in itself marks the Copernican revolution in finance. Simultaneously, given its ability to transform record keeping, the Distributed Ledger is in essence leading us to a new double entry bookkeeping. Actually it is defining Triple Entry bookkeeping: adding a whole new series of layers of proof to the accounting process. In that sense, where the real estate agent has the mantra of "location! Location! Location!" the new era audit is enabled by not sampling or pedantry but direct proof digitised simultaneously across multiple, time stamped, nodes.

Whether we end up with a fully unified system of a buyer's book and a seller's book and so forth that interacts all merchants' transactions, or we still have a vast number of quasi-separate blockchains for these calculations, the simple fact is the use of this private data alongside what will be available on public blockchains concerning issues such as provenance (of product, service, delivery, transport, even IP and more) will provide vast amounts of opportunity for accounts to be better reconciled, compiled faster and indeed become more readily reliable and trusted by investors and all other stakeholders. A distributed ledger, with public and private blocks confirming data can prove there has been no manipulation, error or misrepresentation. In essence, through the judicious use of databots deploying automated approaches (and ultimately Artificial Intelligence), in future the art of spotting the next Bernie Ebbers could prove as easy as throwing on a toga. Even more excitingly it won't require lots of human bodies to do the checking which means a better system at a lower cost – commoditised auditing is coming soon.

It's not just about the accounting but blockchain changes the commercial world just as profoundly as the invention of double entry book keeping transformed society.

Welcome to the new entry of triple entry book keeping – the art of trade by Cotrugli meets the digital scaling of proof and trust enabled by Blockchain.

"We want a whole sequence of companies: digital title, digital media assets, digital stocks and bonds, digital crowdfunding, digital insurance. if you have online trust like the blockchain provides, you can reinvent field after field after field ."

Marc Andreessen

11. Conclusion

"What was valid over 2000 years ago remains valid today. The Romans went to every possible cycle of good and bad, enough to recognize and demonstrate all experiences …. until they stopped living the lessons they learned and eventually were wiped away through their own degenerative behaviors. Things we see in the West are pointing in a direction....."

Marcus Aurelius[1]

We have reached an ideal impasse to conclude – or at least pause – the discussion for now. I have decentralized a body of knowledge. Hopefully you feel emboldened to see in perspective some of the key building blocks shaping our fintech future. Clearly there is much more to discuss...

I have endeavoured to avoid the micro granularities – regtech, proptech or dumbtech. There is no "dumbtech' per se. Albeit having witnessed a voluminous cadre of rubbish pitches in multiple accelerators, I am confused why more people don't use the term as it would be more useful than many hairsplitting diminutives for what all amount to elements of fintech. However, as I said at the very beginning, finance folk are reluctant to be overly transparent and microgranular divisions of what are essentially slices of the same thing are a common foible of those who value opacity over clarity.

The core building blocks we can see. Looking back: the message from history, from Capital Market Revolution! on is clearly one where we can see that transition is inevitable and that change is bringing

---

1. In a new translation (2019) by my good friend and DLT Malta Co Editor, Joseph Antony Debono

huge threats and indeed even greater opportunities to everybody who has the slightest scintilla of intention to engage with the world of finance, whether it is one cent or one satoshi at a time.

As we have seen, network technology drives us all towards markets with a core price for dealing: this is the age of the exchange.

Upon those exchanges yet more products will be developed, as the derivatives world expands...

The derivatives world is clearly maintaining the world of opportunity I have seen for 20 years of Capital Market Revolution!" yet there are also exciting developments for underlying assets too.

Tokenisation underpins the development of every form of investment and can become the very epicentre of money itself. That means reassessing the way money circulates and indeed the Copernican Revolution may be looked upon with horror by the central bankers of today but they are, in essence, a concept whose greatest strength is their own hurbis and proximity to government.

Proximity to government won't save the central bankers any more than it will save the commercial banks from an enormous process of change, albeit their super cycle will take a long time to unwind across centuries. At the same time, it is clear they have been priced out by being 1000 basis points too expensive for the modern networked world.

Amidst talk of a new breed of technology, the blockchain looms large and indeed it may yet see a vast coherence in the auditing field... the joint stock company may outlast the double entry book keeping methods which helped shape our modern broadly prosperous economy.

Again all this analysis has been brought to you by somebody who can only claimed the foresight of a one eyed man, even though at the time of typing my vision for book writing at least, remains firmly binary.

Anyway, I encourage you to make use of the Magic Post It note and to enjoy the view from the peak of banking in the age of the exchange...

When looking at where to go from here, my path has been defined. For in over 70,000 words, 250 something pages and a cornucopia of research, millions of pages have been read, vast numbers of conversations undertaken, thousands of hours of viewing and listening has been undertaken. Yet for all my diligence, I have barely ingested the equivalent of a satoshi or two in relative terms of all the data produced during the time I have been researching.

When a substantive process of research has resulted in only a tiny vestige of all the data generated by the world's markets during the genesis of this book, it provides a clear clue where the future lies.

Therein lies a tail all of its own: for "Victory or Death?" has eschewed a specific discussion of data in this volume for a very simple reason which doesn't require Artificial Intelligence to resolve. A chapter or even two would be insufficient to suitably reduce the key aspects of financial information. Thus the "Capital Market Revolution!" series will return in a tome devoted to big data…

Back in 1999 it all began with a rather tart phrase: "There is nowhere to hide from capital markets. Nobody is safe from the Capital Market Revolution!" The Capital Market Revolution! presents the greatest upheaval ever seen in the fabric of financial markets, and is born of, and driven by, new technology which will ultimately change the lives of every individual on the globe."

Twenty years on there remains only one line to add: Your position in the revolution, whether as an individual or body corporate, remains a binary choice: Victory or Death?

Against that background of ultra competition, it is clear that Austrian economics will shape much of the future of finance (again). As we value the utility of the products, so too the pace of acceleration of change is around us. It's going to be a very long day one out there and we will need to stay ahead to survive the next stage of the Capital Market Revolution! Or to put it in simpler terms:

The only way to deal with Schumpeter is to walk up to a spot of 'creative destruction' and say "Bring it on!"

12. Epilogue

Mahatma Gandhi

China's Alipay network has over 1 billion users every month. By the time you read this there will be around 250 million daily users. It took mankind 200,000 years to reach a billion people on planet Earth. It took Alipay 14 years to reach a billion users.

Take financial data. If we look at the peak of pyramid building in Gizeh (the Great Pyramid was completed circa 2560 BC), through the introduction of rice to Malaysia in 2500 BC, all the way to the Phoenician empire's foundation around a thousand years later... add all their financial data together, then include the markets of Ancient Greece and the entirety of the transactions in the Agora that stretch across the Roman Empire... Indeed roll up everything that occurred in every trading market. Remember Thales of Miletus, the world's first oil derivatives trader...where the lubricant was Olive based. Take every single trade on Tulipmania, the South Sea bubble, the railroad mania, the panics of 1819, 1837, 1857, 1873, 1893... in fact take every panic.

Actually just compress together and compute every last item of financial data produced since we first traded (let's say 2500 BC for the sake of a round number) all the way to 2000 AD, so we have a 4500 year spread of history.

Humankind produced more financial data in the last year than all of those 4500 years. Easily. In fact, we generated around 90% of all data in human history, during the past 2 years.

If you want that in a suitable modern meme, essentially the

population of Kuwait or Kentucky watches a (presumably, cat) video on YouTube every minute, 24*7, 365 days a year.

The world's internet users are still growing at a healthy clip of around 7.5% per annum. Currently 3.7 billion people use a staggering 2.5 quintillion bytes of data daily. There are 18 zeroes in a quintillion, seeing as you asked.

Data usage is deeper and wider while helping us process faster and better across every aspect of our lives but of course the area where the most money to be made is in the world of money itself.

The Revolution continues in data, the Capital Market Revolution! series will return as "Data Never Rests."

About the Author

Patrick L Young wrote the original bestselling book of fintech "Capital Market Revolution!" in 1998 which was published July 1st 1999. A derivatives trader turned fintech pioneer, Patrick's first online business on the web dates back to 1994. He has been an exchange CEO and is a lifelong serial entrepreneur in developed and emerging markets who began his career journey organising old car races in his native Ireland while still at school.

Patrick publishes the daily newsletter of the bourse business "Exchange Invest" and presents the Capital Market Revolution! podcast, amongst others.

In his spare time Patrick is the Chairman of the industry association of the Blockchain Island – Blockchain Malta and the ambassador of the Malta Classic historic motor race meeting which incorporates the Mdina Grand Prix upon which Patrick commentates. Enthusiastically. Born in the North of Ireland, he lives in Valletta with a home in Poland.

Having spoken around the world to conferences and on digital media, Patrick is available for conference keynotes and event chairing as well as advisory work.

You can contact Patrick via: Patrick@DerivativesVision.com.

Index

C

J

London **27, 90, 91, 95, 101, 102, 106, 107, 109, 110, 116, 121, 123, 142, 148**
London Clearing House **101**
London Stock Exchange **102, 109, 110, 123**
LSE **110**
Lubeck **69**
Luca de Pacioli **65**
Luc Bertrand **101**
Lyndon B Johnson **95**

M

Mahwah **89**
Malta **1, 2, 15, 35, 67, 68, 70, 81, 151, 175, 181**
Malthus **5**
Marc Andreessen **174**
Marek Belka **146**
Marino de Raphaeli **69, 163, 166**
Mark Carney **119, 123**
Marriott **165**
Martin Schmidt **117**
Matthew Landry **165**
Mauryan period **35**
Melanie Swan **23**
MercadoLibre **88**
Metro Bank **38**
Mexico **152**
Michael de Guzman **140**
Michael Gove **133**
Microbanking **52**
Microlenders **52**
Microlending **52**
Microsoft **18, 19, 47, 48**
MIFID **53**
Minneapolis **91**

S

USA **18, 19, 47, 56, 91, 94, 101, 148, 149, 152, 153**
USA's (see: USA)
US dollar **94-96, 131, 157**
US Federal Reserve **95**

V

Valletta **1, 67, 181**
VC **89, 149**
Venetian **36, 66, 70**
Venetians (see: Venetian)
Venice **66, 69, 73, 90, 120, 127**
Vernon W Hill II **38**
Verona **90**
Victory or Death **2, 47, 177, 183**
Vimeo **81**
Vitalik Buterin **136**
Vitor Constancio **124**
Vivendi **149**
VOIP **10**

W

Wall Street **89**
Walter Bagehot **122**
Warsaw **103, 110**
Warsaw Stock Exchange **103**
Washington Post **140**
Wei Dai **157**
Western Union **33**
WhatsApp **9**
Whoopi Goldberg **149**
Wieslaw Rozlucki **103**
WiFi Hotspots **9**

William N. Goetzmann **165**
William Paterson **120**
Windows **18**
Worldcom **169**

X

Xenophon **72**

Y

Yale University Press **165**
Young's Pyramid **107, 108**
Youtube **6, 33, 81, 180**
Yu'ebao **132**

Z

Zagreb **110**
Zopa **56**
Zuan de Domenego **69**

Exchange Invest

Exchange Invest

Exchange Invest is the bourse business daily, with the pith of its founder, "Victory or Death?" author Patrick L Young encapsulated under his initials "PLY."

For more details about the unique newsletter of the exchange 'parish' please visit Exchange Invest.com.

Podcast

Podcasts:

The Exchange Invest Weekly is a review of the week in the bourse business selecting key headlines with added pith from the Exchange Invest Newsletter.

The Capital Market Revolution! podcast discusses all manner of topics arising from the Capital Market Revolution! and of course, other books in the series such as Victory or Death? including interviews and discussions with key folks building better markets and investments across the world.